THE DARK SIDE
OF THE DALES

TRUE STORIES OF MURDER, MYSTERY AND ROBBERY FROM THE YORKSHIRE DALES

Best Wishes

Mark,

Mark Bridgeman

Banquo Books

Published in 2024 by

Banquo Books
Scotland
e: banquopublishing@gmail.com

Originally published in 2021 by

Watermill Books
Aberfeldy
www.aberfeldywatermill.com

British Library Cataloguing-in-Publication Data

A catalogue record for this book is available from the British Library

ISBN 978-18381882-4-5

Designed by EMB Graphics, Aberfeldy

Printed and bound in the UK

Cover illustrations by Mark Bridgeman

Internal illustrations by Mark Bridgeman

THE DARK SIDE
OF THE DALES

TRUE STORIES OF MURDER,
MYSTERY AND ROBBERY FROM
THE YORKSHIRE DALES

Mark Bridgeman

Banquo Books

CONTENTS

INTRODUCTION

Rocks! sacred deem'd to eldest fraud, when fear
First darken'd death's reality with dreams!
The spirit of your cruel worship seems,
Like a wolf's shadow, yet to linger here,

From *Brimham Rocks*,
by Yorkshire born poet Ebenezer Elliot (1781-1849)

The raw beauty and rugged splendour of the Yorkshire
Dales is matched by a dark and ominous side. A sinister
and brutal past, where the echoes of evil deeds now hide
in the most picturesque of villages, and the memories
of barbaric crimes lie hidden under craggy, immovable
rocks. Sometimes with a dose of the supernatural to add
an even darker layer. Sometimes even a name can carry a
clue, such as Gibbets Hill near Grassington, where Tom
Lee murdered Dr Petty. Or Dead Man's Hill, named after a
Scottish pedlar murdered in the 18th century, or possibly

after cattle drovers killed by a mother and daughter – it depends on which story you chose to believe.

Throughout the Dales and the market towns and villages that nestle on its borders there are dark and murderous tales to be told. This collection of true stories features crimes that perhaps can teach more about life for the ordinary person during the last 200 years than any history book. Crime gives us a lens through which to view history on a uniquely social and personal level, explaining the struggles of day-to-day life, marriage, illness, misery and even madness. The most mundane characters become the most interesting. Some of the crimes featured here, we hope, could not possibly happen today. Yet many of the themes and motives permeating through the stories in The Dark Side of the Dales – revenge, poverty, drink, greed and anger – are as horribly familiar today as they were a century or two ago.

There are striking differences too. Attitudes to women, to the poor, to alcohol, to mental illness, and to class have shifted to a greater or lesser degree. Yet, many of the social values featured in this collection of stories were so engrained in our culture, that public sympathy often sided with the perpetrator and not the victim.

I have tried wherever possible, to provide a conclusion to the stories. However, there are some tantalising questions that remained unanswered. These, I hope, are balanced by some startling new evidence I have uncovered, together with some possible solutions to two notorious and previously unsolved crimes.

The stories are presented to give an accurate representation of the era, using documented conversations, spellings, and language of the time. I hope this adds to your enjoyment of the stories.

Mark Bridgeman

www.markbridgemanauthor.co.uk

MURDERED FOR MONEY

In early 1905, married mother Martha Smith found employment as a domestic servant at the home of Mr Harold Crossland Shelton in a pleasant four storey Victorian villa in Belle Vue Road in Leeds. Despite having two young children, George and Ivy, aged nine and six, to look after, Martha had been forced into returning to domestic service, to provide for her husband, George Smith. He was a bricklayer by trade, but had been unemployed for a considerable time.

George Smith, now aged 50, seemed content to be out of work, instead demanding that his wife hand over her salary every week to provide him with 'beer money', as well as funds for his gambling. If she argued, or refused, he would lose his temper, often becoming violent both physically and verbally. George Smith considered that his wife's few spare shillings each week were his to do with as he liked. On one occasion Martha's employer Mr Shelton found her crying in a closet, her face bruised and badly cut. On another occasion George Smith burst into Mr Skelton's house demanding yet more money from his wife.

The heated argument disturbed the rest of the household, bringing Mr Shelton's butler into the room. The butler demanded that George Smith leave the house immediately or the police would be called. Furious and red faced, George Smith reluctantly left Belle Vue Road, shouting as he did, 'I'll do for her!'. Martha's employer Mr Skelton regretfully terminated her employment, explaining that he, 'simply could not have a disturbance like that in his house'. He was a considerate employer, however, and knowing the situation was not Martha's fault, he wrote her an excellent reference as a woman employed in domestic service in 1905 could not find employment without one.

Meanwhile, unable to obtain any more money from his wife, George Smith took up lodgings at the house of Mrs Storey in Park Lane, Leeds. Although he had no money or prospects of work, he managed to convince Mrs Storey that his wife would be providing him with money to pay for his board and lodgings. It seems, despite his previous violence towards Martha, she had given him what small amounts of money she could afford during the previous months, even visiting him at his lodgings.

Now unemployed again, Martha Smith went to live with her parents in Wakefield. She did not have to wait long, however, before she found work again. On Saturday 9th September 1905, she left her parents' home to take up a domestic position at the house of a Mr Thomas and Mrs Grace Glendinning in Riddings Road, Ilkley. When Martha arrived, the Glendinnings were away. However, their adult daughter, Miss Catherine Glendinning, greeted Martha and outlined what was expected of her. Martha worked diligently throughout the weekend, cleaning, cooking and stoking the fires. Early on the Tuesday morning, 12th September, Miss Glendinning informed Martha that she would be going to Leeds for the day. She gave Martha two shillings and left at 8 o'clock in the morning. Martha thanked her and set about her duties for the day, which included washing and pressing Mr Glendinning's silk handkerchiefs.

On the same morning, at his lodging in Park Lane, Leeds, George Smith was awake bright and early. He informed his landlady, Mrs Storey, that he would be travelling to Halifax that morning to search for work. Mrs Storey pressed and aired his coat, waistcoat and trousers and he left Leeds at 9.45am. However, George Smith had no intention of going to Halifax and instead journeyed to Ilkley. Smith reached Riddings Road in the early afternoon and asked for directions to the Glendinning's house. A young girl, playing in the street, remembered Smith asking her,

'Is this the street where Miss Glendinning lives?'

'Do you mean Mrs Glendinning?', replied the young girl.

'The house where Mrs Smith is in service'.

The girl pointed to the correct house and Smith thanked her. He then proceeded to walk around to the yard at the back of house. The back door was open and he was witnessed entering the Glenndinning's home, without knocking at approximately 2.30pm by a domestic servant,

Margaret Wilson, who was working in the neighbouring house. At 4.00pm Margaret Wilson, looking through the windows of the neighbouring house, noticed Martha Smith hanging out washing in the Glenndinning's back yard.

Margaret Wilson also noticed a man leaning against the open door frame of the rear door to the house, watching Martha. He was talking, but the witness was unable to discern what he was saying. When Martha had finished hanging out the washing she went back inside the house. It was to be the last confirmed sighting of her.

Miss Glendinning returned at 6.30pm in the evening and entered through the front door, which was unlocked. The sun was beginning to set behind the houses to the west. She called out for Martha but received no answer. Walking through to the rear of the house she tried the back door, in case Martha had been in back yard and not heard her calling. The door was locked from the inside. Miss Glendinning called out Martha's name again and decided to check the cellar kitchen when she received no answer. On entering the cellar, there in front of her was the body of a woman slumped and twisted on the tiles, covered in blood. The upper part of the torso was facing the wall and the legs were resting against the water heater (known as a 'copper'). The floor was a crimson red and there were other signs of a violent struggle. After recovering from the initial shock, Miss Glendinning ran up the cellar stairs and fetched Margaret Wilson from the house next door. They lifted the head of the body and, realising it was Martha Smith, sent for the police and a doctor.

On arrival Dr Thomas Hearder examined the body which he noted was cold, meaning that Martha Smith had probably died within minutes of her last confirmed sighting at 4pm. Despite having witnessed many victims of violence Dr Hearder was shocked by the savagery of the attack. There were no less than 49 separate wounds on Martha's body. The most severe injury being a slashed wound across the victim's neck measuring three and a half inches in length and penetrating Martha's throat to a depth of two and a half inches. It was clear to Dr Hearder that this wound alone was enough to have caused death. A collection of defensive wounds on Martha's arms, hands, fingers, and wrists indicated that she had vainly attempted to defend herself against her attacker. The doctor confirmed to the police that a sharp instrument, probably a knife, had been used in the attack; and that the assailant had used extreme force.

Police constables questioned residents of Riddings Road and it soon became clear that the estranged husband of the victim was the prime suspect. He had been seen entering the house, although no one had seen him leave. Indeed, he may well have still been in the house when Catherine Glendinning returned; slipping away unnoticed while Miss Glendinning was in the cellar. Officers from Ilkley police called on George Smith's lodgings in Park Lane, Leeds, and arrested him. Smith was evidently not expecting the police to trace him so quickly, for he had not changed his clothes. The knees of his trousers were bloodstained and his waistcoat and shirt were soaked with blood. Most tellingly of all, a silk handkerchief belonging to Mr Glendinning was found in Smith's pocket. In addition, a sum of one shilling and seven pence was found, together with two heartbreaking letters written to him by his wife.

George Smith was formerly charged with the murder of his wife and brought to trial at Leeds Crown Court in December 1905. Mr Harold Thomas and Mr RA Shepherd appeared for the prosecution. Smith was defended by Mr EH Chapman.

The prosecution felt their case was a simple matter of proving Smith's movements on the day of the murder. Several witnesses were produced who testified to seeing Smith in Riddings Road on the afternoon of the crime. Martha Smith's former employer, Mr Shelton, and two further witnesses, were able to attest to George Smith's previous violent conduct towards his wife. The two letters written by Martha, and found in her husband's possession at the time of his arrest, were produced in court:

George,

I wish you had not taken that money. It has caused me a lot of trouble this week. I cannot sleep for thinking about it, and I do hope you will try and pay it back, for I cannot see what I can do towards it. Aren't you ashamed of yourself that me and the children had to go and sleep by other people's firesides? I heard tell of your having a row with that woman and our Jenny, and I was much grieved. I expect you are carrying a nice game on now. You may well want me out of the way. George and Ivy keep asking if you are living with 'Long Poll'.

So good-bye, and may God Almighty bless you – Your wife in name only, MS

A second letter was produced by the prosecution in which Martha Smith recounted being forced to beg for food and clothes for herself and the children. She concluded the letter:

My dear George, - I wish you had some work, for I am tired of thinking. With kind love to you, and may God help you to be a better man.

The most damming piece of evidence was saved until last, however. George Smith's landlady, Mrs Storey, confirmed that a small butcher's knife had gone missing from her house on the morning of the murder. She first noticed its absence shortly after Smith had left for the day, claiming he was going to Halifax.

The prosecution rested and Mr EH Chapman rose from his seat to begin the defence. Smith had pleaded 'not guilty', claiming that he could not remember murdering his wife. He stood in the dock and made a statement to the court, the ability for the accused to speak in his own defence being a relatively new and novel experience in 1905:

Martha was a widow when I married her, eleven years ago, and our home was broken up owing to my being out of work. She was a kind and affectionate wife, and provided me with some of the money she earned.

Smith denied taking the butcher's knife from his lodgings but did admit to carrying a small penknife with him. He continued to describe the events of the 12th September, explaining that his wife gave him a drink of beer and a sandwich, upon his arrival at the house in Riddings Road. An argument ensued in which Smith grabbed Martha and, under cross-examination, his version of the events emerged.

'I don't want you to touch me,' begged Martha, 'I don't want you anymore. I have got someone else now.'

Smith grabbed her roughly and threatened, 'I will take my children from Wakefield'. She pushed him back yelling 'Get away; I don't want to have any more to do with you.'

Smith told the court, 'I had my penknife and I went for her, and she went for me. She took up a piece of board and hit me on the shoulder with it. We had a struggle, and I dug the penknife at her.'

Lord Justice Arthur Jelf, the presiding Judge, interjected at this point, 'Had she any sharp instrument?'

'I don't know.'

'Now be careful what you say', observed Lord Jelf

'I don't think she had, sir. She dragged the penknife from my hand.'

'Was it a result of what she said that you went for her?'

'Yes', came Smith's answer, 'I am very short tempered'.

Under cross-examination by Mr Thomas, Smith admitted to being very angry at Martha's suggestion that he had been 'carrying on with another woman'. He acknowledged having known a woman nicknamed 'Long Poll' for two years; but denied being intimate with her. He also confessed to throwing Martha to the floor during the argument, to having given her a black eye, and to the fact that she was so terrified she had hidden behind a clothes horse in the cellar at Riddings Road.

Smith's answers under cross-examination were contradictory and incriminating. He admitted to taking the butcher's knife from his lodgings, after first having denied it, but claimed that he subsequently threw it away. Mr Thomas continued to press Smith,

'How did you get the blood upon your clothes?'

'I stayed with her to the finish. I kissed her, and she kissed me. I lifted her out of the blood, and put her in the position where she was found.'

'Do you remember inflicting the wound to her neck?'

I did not do one so long as that.'

Mr Thomas pressed Smith again, 'Do you say you did it or not?'

'I certainly did it.'

'But before that, you had inflicted upon her over 40 other wounds!'

Smith motioned with his arm, striking down as if holding a knife, 'I just kept going like that.' A horrified gasp echoed around the court room.

'Had she any means of defending herself?'

'Her hands'

'I put it to you that she had no means of defending herself!'

'Yes', Smith replied, 'but she started the bother with me first.'

Following this damning cross-examination the prosecution summed up their case to the jury. His previous treatment of the victim, his attempts 'to throw a slur upon the poor woman's character' and the theft of the butcher's knife all indicated 'malice aforethought', the prosecution alleged.

The defence addressed the jury, reminding them that they were not obliged to find the prisoner guilty of murder. If they believed that 'the frenzy of madness was upon the man, he was no longer able to answer the voice of reason and was entitled to clemency.' Mr Chapman also submitted that any circumstance of provocation by his wife would enable them to find the prisoner guilty of the lesser offence of manslaughter.

The jury, however, was not to be swayed. In less than fifteen minutes they returned with a unanimous verdict of guilty of murder.

Lord Jelf donned his black cap and pronounced sentence on George Smith, who sat impassively in the dock:

George Smith, you have been found guilty on the clearest evidence of one of the most brutal murders it has ever been my lot to try. If anything could have added to your wickedness, it was your attempt to cast aspersions on your wife's character. I am of the opinion that she was a good, kind wife, and it was very sad to think that you should have so cruelly treated her.

The sentence of this court is that you will be taken from here to the place from whence you came, and from there that you be taken to the place of execution and there hanged by the neck until you are dead. And may God have mercy upon your soul.

There was to be no reprieve for George Smith. He was executed at Leeds Jail, on 28th December 1905 by Britain's senior Public Executioner Henry Pierrepoint. Smith's body was taken and buried within the grounds of the prison.

THE CATTLE MART KILLER

The weather in March 1932 had been atrocious. Farmers in the Dales were desperate for an improvement to assist with lambing. Meanwhile the public were coming to terms with the new Import Duties Act, which had brought price rises of 10% or more to the shops.

Joseph Swaine was a popular farmer from Otley and was well known in Wharfedale farming circles. He had recently rented a farmhouse and land adjacent to the Otley golf course. Swaine was planning to marry a local Otley girl, Miss Gwendolen Forrest, in the near future. The couple had been involved for several years, despite their huge age difference. He was 62, she was 25 – a fact that would be speculated upon by the press over the coming weeks. Joseph Swaine shared an early evening meal with Gwendolen on the evening of Tuesday 22nd March, at her attractive Victorian terraced house in Queen's Terrace. After eating, he informed her that he would be travelling to Skipton for the farmers' auction mart, which was due to take place on the following day. He intended to set out that evening by bus, as he wished to break his journey by visiting a friend, Fred Deighton, in Addingham, along the way. The two men then intended to travel to the auction mart together the following morning. Joseph Swaine said goodnight to his sweetheart and promised her he would be back the following evening.

The Skipton Auction Mart had been extremely busy, with farmers from across Yorkshire in attendance. After a busy morning viewing livestock and chatting to other farmers and bidders, during which time there were many confirmed sightings of Swaine, he seems to have vanished during the afternoon. He was last seen by a witness going into the mens' lavatory at some point between 2.45pm and 3.30pm. The witness also noticed a group of three men stood close to the lavatory door around the time that Swaine entered. The witness could not describe the men; or be more precise as to the time. No one could remember seeing Swaine leave the lavatory, which was in an outbuilding at the rear of the premises and not overlooked.

Gwendolen Forrest waited for Joseph but he did not return in the evening from the Mart. She later said, 'When he did not come, I imagined that he might have been hurt in a bus smash, or something of the sort, and I fretted all night'. She did not, however, call the police or Mr Pickard, the landlord at Chevin Lodge in Otley, where Swaine lodged.

The following morning, Thursday 24th March, at around 9am, a cleaner entered the lavatory at the Skipton Auction Mart. Initially nothing seemed out of place in the dingy,

poorly lit room. The floor was wet and muddy, but that
was to be expected after the heavy rain of the previous few
days. Unusually, the cleaner then noticed, a pair of false
teeth had been placed carefully on the window ledge above
the urinal. They appeared quite dirty and the cleaner
assumed that the owner must have dropped them without
realising, only for the next person to place them on the
shelf. As the cleaner mopped the floor of the lavatory he
noticed a stream of blood flowing from under the door
of the furthest cubicle from the entrance. However, he
was unable to open the door which seemed to be jammed
shut. With a tremendous effort he pushed the door, which
begrudgingly swung open. The door had been locked
from the inside and had also been partially blocked by the
slumped body of Joseph Swaine. Barely alive, he had clearly
suffered a huge and traumatic head injury. The employee
raced away to fetch the police and the doctor, but Swaine
died shortly afterwards.

The police reacted quickly and Detective Superintendent
Blacker and Superintendent Hodgson from Otley took
charge. Swaine's body was identified by employees of the
Mart where he was a regular visitor and the police quickly
surmised that Swaine had been attacked and hit from
behind across the right side of his head by a heavy, blunt
object with enough force to fracture his skull and send
his false teeth ricocheting across the room. This meant
his attacker was probably right-handed. The body was
then dragged into the cubicle, to conceal the crime. The
assailants had then locked the cubicle door from the inside
and climbed out over the top of the stall. When Joseph

Swaine's body was discovered he had lain undetected for approximately 18 hours, bleeding from the severe head injury. The concrete floor and walls of the cubicle were covered with blood, as were Swaine's hands, where he had attempted unsuccessfully to raise himself. Detectives could not find a wallet in Swaine's pockets or on the floor. Robbery appeared to be the motive, although his pocket watch had not been taken.

Evidence was gathered from as many witnesses as possible and a statement was issued to the local press:

MURDER - £100 REWARD.

About 9am on Thursday, 24 March, 1932, Joseph Swaine, aged 62, of Otley, was found in a dying condition in a lavatory at the Skipton Auction Mart. He had been brutally assaulted about the head, and died shortly after he was found. On the previous day the deceased was seen about 3.15pm in the Auction Mart, and was probably attacked shortly after that time. He was robbed of a brown pocket-book, some Treasury notes, a Barclay's Bank cheque book, and a cheque for £5 10s. drawn in favour of the Midland Bank. A reward of £100 (approximately £7,000 today) is offered to any person who will give information leading to the conviction of the murderer or murderers.

(Signed) F Brook Chief Constable

The police had little to go on, however, robbery seemed the obvious motive. Gwendolen Forrest concurred with the detectives, telling them that, 'it was Joseph's custom to carry a fairly large amount of money with him, and only two or three days ago he showed me a number of notes. There would have been at least £10 (about £700 today), and probably more. Robbery is the only thing it could possibly be'.

Skipton Auction Mart, and other similar gatherings, were a haven for 'pickpockets, tricksters, and welshers', according to the Skipton Police. Undercover police officers attended the Gisburn Point-to-Point race meeting, and the Pendle Forest Hunt, hoping to catch the killer as he searched for another victim, but they were unable to locate any possible suspects.

A search of nearby allotments was made for the murder weapon and an accurate timeline of Swaine's movements was quickly established. A witness confirmed seeing Joseph Swaine sitting in the store cattle ring at the Auction Mart shortly before 3pm. This appears to be the last time that anyone saw him alive. Distressingly, it also transpired that several witnesses had noticed blood on the floor of the lavatory after 3.30pm; but had not reported it. Another witness reported that Joseph Swaine had complained of feeling unwell, which perhaps accounted for his false teeth being placed so carefully on the window ledge. Perhaps he had taken them out and, whilst bent over the sink, had been struck from behind?

Detectives were also puzzled by the audacity of the crime, taking place as it did while the cattle sales were in full flow and hundreds of farmers and breeders were present. This led the police to speculate that more than one person was involved in the attack. Perhaps a second man was employed as a lookout while the attack took place?

Meanwhile, the police spread the parameters of their search, questioning drivers in the Otley area and further afield. A press conference was arranged, in which they appealed for further information, 'There must have been a number of people at the cattle market at that time, within a few feet of the spot where the man was found. Someone must have noticed him'.

Other leads were pursued. A bundle of bloodstained clothing was discovered in a field at Horton-in-Ribbledale, a few miles north of Skipton. Bloodhounds were even employed to trace the scent; but after following it for several miles eventually lost the scent in a patch of woodland. The bloodstained clothing would later prove to be unrelated.

On 10th April the police released the descriptions of three men seen loitering outside the lavatory on the day Joseph Swaine was murdered. The first man was described as 5ft 6in tall, aged about 28, with fair hair and light flannel trousers. The second man as being about 5ft 4in tall, aged about 24, with dark hair and two-three days' growth of beard, wearing dark blue overalls and army boots. The third man was described as 5ft 5in, aged about 40, with dark brown hair and two-three days growth of beard, and wearing muddy black boots. One of the trio was said to have been wearing a dirty mackintosh and another was thought to have been Irish.

It was reported that they were believed to have purchased railway tickets from Hawes in North Yorkshire to Hawes Junction on the day after the murder and then purchased tickets to Ulverston. A witness stated that, whilst at Hawes, they had asked how far it was to Barrow-in-Furness, as well as the distance to Barnard Castle, and had remarked that they had wanted to make the journey across the moors.

Following the police appeal they were tracked down in the North Yorkshire Moors. However, after interviewing the three men, they were able to satisfy the detectives as to their innocence. Another potential lead had proved fruitless. The police would have to start from scratch.

A further two weeks passed without a breakthrough in the case. The public were concerned that a violent killer was on the loose, while senior officers demanded daily updates from the harassed detectives. Finally, on 1st May, a breakthrough came in the investigation. Detective Inspector Bates, of Bradford City Police, received a communication from a man named John Blanchfield. It appeared that Blanchfield had recently been in conversation with a drifter named Thomas Gaunt. Gaunt had boasted about the Skipton Murder, claiming he had hit Joseph Swaine over the head with a crowbar. Gaunt, aged 24, was a collier, from a mining family in Clowne, Derbyshire. However, he was currently unemployed and of no fixed abode, wandering around the towns and villages of the Dales. Those who had witnessed him all spoke of his erratic nature. Police officers traced Gaunt to a dingy Bradford hostel, where he had been staying, and he was brought to Skipton Police Station to be questioned by Detective Winter.

Initially, under questioning, Gaunt blurted out, 'It's that Skipton murder. I hit him on the head with a crowbar and dragged him into the lavatory. My friend got his wallet, then gave me my share'. Pressured by the police officers, Gaunt refused to reveal the name of the other man. When asked to make a statement Gaunt replied, 'it's your bloody job now'. Detectives decided to formally charge Thomas Gaunt with the murder of Joseph Swaine, which would allow them more time to investigate their new suspect. On being asked if he wished to answer the charge, he simply replied, 'Tell them I did it'.

Thomas Gaunt was clearly an unbalanced individual, with a highly volatile character. It was decided to order a medical examination while he was on remand at Armley Jail, in Leeds. Dr John Humphrey, the Medical Officer at the Jail, informed the magistrates that he regarded Gaunt as legally certifiable under the Lunacy Act. Dr Humphrey had kept Gaunt under observation for a period of two weeks, and also considered evidence of his previous behaviour. Gaunt, it transpired, had two previous arrests for violence and a long history of apoplexy (the definition of which in the 1920s meant an incapacity of cerebral capacity, perhaps caused by a stroke or haemorrhage, resulting in unpredictable behaviour). During his time under medical examination Gaunt had a number of apoplectic fits, usually at night. Gaunt was described as 'unstable in his mind, for long periods and suffering from terrifying dreams. He did not know whether they were realities or dreams'. Gaunt also told the doctor he was under the impression that he was 'an agent sent by God to help people that were down and out by giving them sixpences'. These feelings were then followed by a deep depression during which time God taunted him, 'you are a scoundrel, a blackguard and a scapegrace (a wayward person).' Gaunt also informed the doctor that he had previously purchased rat poison with the intention to kill himself. However, at the last moment his courage had failed him and he had been unable to go through with it.

The police were unable to corroborate any of Gaunt's claims regarding the killing of Joseph Swaine. It also proved impossible to pinpoint his movements on the day of the killing; nor were they able to trace the murder weapon and compare fingerprints. Despite his admission of guilt, Gaunt was evidently unable to comprehend the charges brought against him, or of facing trial in a court of law. He was discharged into the care of staff at the huge Menston Mental Asylum Hospital. The hospital, at that time, was a largely self-sufficient institution, with its own library, surgery, dispensary, butchery, dairies, bakery, shop, and cobbler's workshops, on a large estate partly devoted to agriculture and market gardening. The patients lived in wards and if they were able, were expected to work towards their keep either on the farm, in the kitchens or laundry, or in various handicraft facilities. Menston even boasted its own small railway system, which was connected to the main Wharfedale Railway Line. The hospital, which would later be involved in the scandal surrounding Jimmy Savile, eventually closed in 2003. Hospital records regarding the subsequent treatment and life of Thomas Gaunt are sealed under the '100 Year Rule' and will not be made available until at least 2032.

Although Thomas Gaunt confessed to the killing of Joseph Swaine, his admission of guilt could never be accepted in a court of law. As a result, the case remains technically unsolved to this day. No one else has ever been tried for the murder of Joseph Swaine and subsequently no other avenues were explored by the police, nor were any other suspects actively pursued.

Joseph Swaine was buried at Otley Parish Church in front of a large crowd of mourners, who comforted his grieving fiancée.

THE WHARFEDALE TRUNK MYSTERY
(PART ONE)

It was a dark and inclement night during the winter of late 1891, or possibly early 1892. A young woman, wrapped in a long shawl to protect herself from the elements and to partially conceal the small round tin chest she was carrying, made her way silently along the roadway between Buckden and Kettlewell, in a secluded part of Upper Wharfedale.

Distraught in appearance, the young woman was grateful that the inky black night obscured her troubled expression from anyone who happened to pass by. As she walked alone, carrying a carpet bag on one arm, and holding the tin chest under her shawl with the other arm, she glanced furtively behind her and from left to right, peering over the low, dry stone walls that lined the road.

Eventually she reached the hamlet of Starbotton, flanked by sharply rising hills distinctively silhouetted against the night sky. Its name was derived from the Norse word 'botn' meaning 'a depth'. The young woman had recently moved into a small cottage at Horner's Farm, following her marriage to a farmhand who was employed there. Her husband's brother also lodged in the cottage with them.

However, instead of returning to her new home in the farm cottage, and to her husband, she made her way carefully and quietly into the farmyard; guided by a sliver of moonlight from a clear sky. The farm was silent and the yard was not overlooked. The occupant of the main farmhouse, a farmer named Anthony Horner, had long since retired for the night.

Looking around, she noticed a pile of rubbish, ashes and dirt which had accumulated over a long period of time in a hollowed out recess under the stone steps leading to the granary. The young woman carefully removed the small tin chest from underneath her garments. Securing the lid tight shut with a small padlock, she then wrapped the chest carefully in newspapers and buried it deep into the heap of refuse, making sure that she covered it again, carefully ensuring that the pile of refuse appeared to be undisturbed. With another cautious glance around her, to make sure she had not woken the occupants of the farmhouse, she returned to the small cottage where her new husband was asleep in bed. She tossed the padlock key over a drystone wall into the field as she hurried back home, then carefully opened the door, so as not to wake her husband.

The following morning, she explained away her late return on the previous evening by telling her husband that she had received a letter from her brother in Bishop Thornton, requesting that she visit him urgently on family business. After leaving a hastily written note for her husband on the mantelpiece, explaining the need to travel to Bishop Thornton, she had set out immediately via the thirty miles of winding lanes, rolling hills and breezy moorlands.

It is not known whether she had taken the small, tin chest with her from the farm cottage, and taken it to Bishop Thornton, or whether she had acquired it while journeying to her brother's. However, on her return home, its absence from the house was not noticed or remarked upon. The secret of the mysterious tin chest was forgotten, and life continued as normal, until one summer's day years later.

The new century dawned, Queen Victoria passed away in 1901 and her son was crowned as King Edward VII. The war against the Boers had commenced in the colonies of southern Africa and, by 1905, the horse drawn parcel posts and coaches that served the Dales were being replaced by the first motorised lorries. The British Red Cross had been recently founded, and Emily Pankhurst had led the first Suffragettes' protest.

Meanwhile, Mr Anthony Horner, the owner of the farm at Starbotton, had employed a workman to dig some drainage trenches on his farmland and to undertake some general maintenance. On Tuesday 4th July, 1905, the workman began to clear the rubbish pile that had collected over many years underneath the steps to the granary. Pushing down deep into the heap of rubbish and ashes, his shovel made a sharp metallic clang as its progress was

temporarily halted by something solid and unyielding.
Investigating further, he scraped the ashes and dirt to one
side to reveal an old, rusty, round tin chest. The chest was
dirty, covered in the accrued grime of many years.

Brushing the grime aside with his sleeve, he could see the
box had rusted with age, but was still securely padlocked.
The workman noticed that it was the type of small chest
commonly used by female domestic servants in the Dales.
He carefully lifted up the chest. As he did, the rusted and
decayed bottom gave way and the contents spilled out onto
the ground in front of him.

Inside the small chest were the decomposed remains of
a small child. Wrapped in a light-coloured knitted shawl,
the body had almost completely decayed. Just the skull
remained intact. Next to the remains of the body were a
pair of small child's shoes and a pair of child's gaiters. One
other item fell out of the chest, a small empty bottle of
what appeared to be the type used to dispense poison.

Horrified, the workman recoiled. After fighting back the
urge to be violently sick, he gathered his composure,
jumped up and ran to fetch Mr Horner, who in turn sent
for Dr Wilks, Police-Sergeant Hardwick from Grassington
and Mr Edgar Wood, the County Coroner. On visiting the
gruesome scene Mr Wood, the Coroner, called an urgent
inquiry to be held at Starbotton, which opened on the
following day.

Dr Wilks reported to the inquest that the body had clearly
been buried for some considerable time, undoubtedly

years, and that the child was probably eighteen months old at the time of death, based on the size of the shoes. Due to the state of decomposition, he was unable to determine the child's sex, but could say that the child had been dressed (although what remained of the clothing had largely disintegrated), then wrapped in a light-coloured, or possibly white, shawl. The small tin chest or trunk, he thought, was of the type commonly used by girls in domestic service, a similar opinion to the workman who found the body. The inquest was adjourned until 18th August 1905 and the Skipton Police were instructed to begin their investigations. Although, with little to go on, and a considerable passage of time having elapsed since the tin chest had been hidden, they had little hope of making any immediate progress. However, with no Statute of Limitation for the act of murder, the importance of investigating the crime had not diminished over time.

Meanwhile, speculation was rife in the neighbourhood. Many people remembered the young woman who had moved into Starbotton, then disappeared suddenly. The story appeared in newspapers across the county under the lurid headline 'The Wharfedale Trunk Mystery'. It was not long before the innkeeper of the Chequers Inn at Bishop Thornton, Mr Henry Rawson, heard the tragic tale. Something about the story brought to mind a sequence of events that had occurred 15 years earlier. He visited Skipton Police Station and made a statement to Superintendent Lumb, detailing the following sequence of events.

On 18th May 1890, his sister Alice Rawson had given
birth to a baby daughter at the Chequers' Inn. Alice was
unmarried and the pregnancy had been a closely guarded
secret, for fear of disgrace in the family. It appears that
not even Richard Rawson, Alice's father, knew of her

condition. Following the birth, the baby girl was given
the name Ida Wiseman Rawson. The conventions of the
time meant that the child could not be brought up by an
unmarried mother. Ida was given to a widowed lady, well
known to the Rawsons, who agreed to nurse her until such
time as Alice had married and would be able to reclaim
her daughter – providing of course that any prospective
husband would agree to taking on such a child.

Alice Rawson was sent away to the quiet hamlet of
Starbotton, to avoid any scandal or gossip, and found a
position there as a domestic servant. She settled into a

working routine and the child remained a secret. She did not mention her baby to a living soul, for fear of disgrace and of losing her position. Still only 23 years old, her family hoped she could find a suitable husband, and put her troubled past behind her. Before long she met a farmer's son, Christopher Parrington, who was living and working nearby. Three years older than Alice, he was a hard-working and honest man. Within a short while the couple were engaged, and the date of their marriage was announced. Soon afterwards, on 17th December 1891, Alice married Christopher Parrington at St Michael's Church in Linton-in-Craven and the couple moved into a cottage at Horner's farm in Starbotton, where Christopher and his brother worked.

On hearing of the wedding, Alice's brother Henry wrote to her and requested that, now that she was legally married, she should return to Bishop Thornton immediately and take her seven-month-old daughter back home with her. Alice agreed and duly arrived at The Chequers Inn to reclaim her daughter. Her brother helped her gather together all of the child's belongings and accompanied the newly reacquainted mother and daughter to Ripley Railway Station, from where he believed Alice and her daughter were travelling onwards to Harrogate. That was the last occasion, 15 years previously, that he had seen or heard from his sister, nor had he heard anything regarding the daughter, Ida, who he now believed would be about 15 years old. Superintendent Lumb listened to the strange story with incredulity, perhaps doubting that the child had ever existed. Henry Rawson took a folded piece of paper from his pocket, it was Ida's Certificate of Birth dated 18th May 1890.

The Superintendent instigated a series of enquiries with other police forces in the county and with Somerset House in London (where, at the time, all records of births, deaths and marriages were stored). Initially, they had some trouble tracing Alice, who had taken to calling herself Alice Chapman (her husband's middle name). The couple had moved from Starbotton a year or so after Alice's return from her trip to Bishop Thornton. They appear to have then spent time in Lancashire and Coal Aston in Derbyshire, before settling at 64 Nettleham Road in Sheffield, where Christopher had taken up work as a builder's labourer.

The police could find no record of a young girl called Ida ever having lived at Nettleham Road, or anywhere else. In fact, according to neighbours at Coal Aston in Derbyshire and Nettleham Road in Sheffield, Christopher and Alice Parrington's first daughter was not born until 1893; and the child's name was Ann. A check of the 1901 Census records showed that the Parrington family consisted of husband Christopher (aged 38), his wife Alice Marion (35), and two daughters, Ann (8), and May (6). A further child, Phyllis, was born in 1902. There was no mention of Ida, who seemed to have vanished from the face of the earth. No witnesses could be located who could ever remember seeing the child.

This information convinced the police, and Sergeant

Hardwick was dispatched to Sheffield. At 9.30pm on the first Saturday of August in 1905, he knocked sharply on the door of 64 Nettleham Road. Alice Parrington opened the door.

'Alice Marion Parrington?', queried Sergeant Hardwick.

She answered, 'yes, that's me, why?'.

'Alice Marion Parrington, also known as Alice Rawson or Chapman, I am arresting you on the suspicion of the murder of your illegitimate child, Ida Wiseman Rawson, at Starbotton, during the latter part of 1890, or the early part of 1891.'

Alice was initially taken to Skipton Police Station, where she was questioned. She denied ever having had a child before marriage. Sergeant Hardwick produced Ida's birth certificate but Alice still denied having had a baby before she was married. She claimed to have never seen the document before, telling Sergeant Hardwick it must be a forgery. She was then taken to Armley Jail in Leeds to await the first committal hearing.

A formal magistrates' hearing was held on the 18th August. Alice appeared fraught and anxious, although the hearing only lasted a few minutes. It was quickly decided to rearrange proceedings for 18th October to allow the police further time to investigate the case. The resulting hearing at Skipton Town Hall on 18th October aroused huge public interest and an enormous jostling throng gathered in the street, many of them queueing from the early hours. In fact, many of the locals gathered outside, on seeing the size and raucous nature of the crowd, wrongly believed that an afternoon's musical entertainment was being presented instead!

Scores of police officers were busily employed all day calming the volatile audience outside the Town Hall. Magistrates Colonel Robinson, the treasurer of Skipton Town Council, and Mr Thomas Dewhurst, the local mill owner, presided. Mr G. Robinson appeared as the Public Prosecutor and Mr A. Willey, a solicitor from Leeds, represented Alice Parrington. Due to the large number of people gathered outside, the prudent decision was made to hold the hearing behind closed doors. Only a handful of officials and newspaper reporters were allowed inside. Police officers remained outside and a promise was made to the expectant crowd that an announcement would be made on the steps of the Town Hall, following the conclusion of the hearing.

Meanwhile, inside the Town Hall the specially arranged hearing was about to begin.

THE WHARFEDALE TRUNK MYSTERY
(PART TWO)

Presiding magistrate Thomas Dewhurst opened the second hearing to determine if sufficient evidence existed to order court proceeding against Alice Parrington for the murder of her eighteen-month-old daughter Ida, fifteen years earlier. It had been two months since the earlier magistrates' hearing and the public were anxious for answers.

Unlike the previous magistrates' inquiry, held on the 18th August, there was a marked difference in Alice's demeanour. This time she presented a composed and calm exterior to the court, some observers noting that she appeared almost distracted and disinterested. The Yorkshire Post reported that 'while all the preliminaries were settled, she contented herself in reading the literature which adorns the walls. She was dressed in a dark, tight-fitting costume, and wore a tiller hat.'

Mr Robinson spoke for the Crown, announcing that:

The authorities in London had carefully considered all the circumstances and the time that had elapsed since the birth of the prisoner's illegitimate child, in May 1890, and the finding of the decomposed remains of a child at Horner's Farm, Starbotton. Furthermore, the difficulty in identifying either the body, or the clothes it had worn. Neither had it been possible to trace the owner of the trunk in which the remains were found. Under the circumstances, the Public Prosecutor did not think the evidence was such as to warrant the magistrates committing the prisoner for trial. Accordingly, I am instructed not to offer any further evidence, and to ask that the prisoner be discharged.

Mr Willey, for the defence, agreed, noting that the only evidence against his client seemed to be the word of her brother, who had not seen her for 15 years and who struggled to even recognise her at the first Magistrates' hearing in August.

The Magistrate, Thomas Dewhurst, agreed, 'Under the circumstances there is no other course of action but to discharge the accused on the grounds of insufficient evidence'. He turned to Alice Parrington, 'You have heard what Mr Robinson has said?'

'Yes, sir'.

You are discharged'.

'Thank you, sir'.

With that, the two prison warders, who had stood impassively on either side of Alice during the hearing, moved aside and her freedom was officially granted by Mr

Thomas Dewhurst.

Meanwhile the crowd gathered in the High Street outside the Town Hall had begun to grow impatient. Their chanting and shouting gradually grew to a crescendo. It was decided by the officials present that an announcement should be made to the impatient throng. Mr Dewhurst and Colonel Robinson came out onto the balcony and declared to the crowd that there would be no further trial, due to insufficient evidence, and that Mrs Alice Parrington was free to leave. Their pronouncement was greeted with a mixed reaction, there was some cheering and some booing, but generally the result was not entirely unexpected. The crowd began to slowly drift away, and it seems that Alice was able to return to Sheffield without being subjected to any unpleasant or ugly scenes (at least, none were reported in the press). She was escorted from the Town Hall by her solicitor, Mr Willey, and returned to Sheffield to her husband.

The murder of the infant interred in a tin chest and buried in a pile of rubbish remains technically unsolved to this day. As does the cause of death. Although poisoning was always thought to be the most likely, bearing in mind that what appeared to be a poison bottle was discovered alongside the remains of the child.

However, there still seem to be more questions than answers in this tragic case. Did Alice Parrington murder her unwanted child, in order to keep her indiscretion secret from her husband? Was it possible that her husband was actually fully aware of the child and agreed to the disposal of the body? The matter certainly does not appear to have ever been investigated fully. The evidence of the birth certificate seems to have been largely ignored, as does Alice's blatant lie in denying the existence of an illegitimate child.

Her husband's brother (Edmund Parrington, a carrier by trade) lodged with Alice and her husband Christopher for two years following their marriage. He stated at the inquest that he could not recollect her ever bringing a tin box or chest into the house. He was also certain that Alice did not return from Bishop Thornton that night with a baby, nor was any previous child ever mentioned. He went further, putting on the record that, 'in fact, I was not aware she had had a child before marriage until recently.' Edmund Parrington's statement seems to exonerate his brother's part in the sordid affair.

What is known for certain, nevertheless, is that Ida Wiseman Rawson was born on 18th May 1890 and disappeared seven months later, never to be seen alive again. She left Bishop Thornton in the arms of the mother in late 1890 and vanished. No other child was reported missing in the area and the body found in the tin chest was never presumed to be the remains of anyone else. No appeals were made to try and identify the child, nor did anyone else come forward with a possible alternative. Not a single other possible missing infant was suggested or even investigated by the police. Perhaps this was simply a case that everyone hoped would best be forgotten.

It seemed to many locals as if potential damage to the region's burgeoning tourist trade necessitated a quick resolution, with the minimum possible fuss and publicity and at the expense of justice. However, this did not prevent news of the case spreading far and wide. The story of the tragedy cascaded from local to national newspapers, eventually being reported as far away as Australia.

As for Christopher and Alice Parrington, their marriage seemed to have survived the scandal, which strongly suggests that Alice's husband simply did not believe the accusations against his wife, choosing instead to believe her version of events. However, the sensation surrounding the case did force the couple to move from Sheffield to the quieter town of Barnoldswick, some 70 miles away. Christopher obtained further work as a builder and the couple rented a small, terraced cottage; number 15 East Street, a narrow street of traditional workers' cottages. The couple had one more daughter, Zena, born in 1909. They appear to have lived a quiet life following the sensation caused by the 'Wharfedale Trunk Mystery'.

As an intriguing footnote, during my research for this story I uncovered some startling documents, which both add credence to Henry Rawson's version of events; and proves that Alice's claim, that she had not previously given birth to a daughter before getting married in December 1891, was a complete fabrication. Firstly, tucked away at the bottom of page 29, in the 'Records for Baptisms solemnized in the Parish of Bishop Thornton, in the diocese of Ripon, for 1890', is the formal entry for the baptism of Ida Wiseman Rawson, which took place on 12th

October. Listed as present was the mother 'Alice Marion Rawson, Spinster, from Shaw Mills, Bishop Thornton. Officiating Minister JJ Lucas'.

Secondly, the birth of Ida Wiseman Rawson was, indeed, registered in Pateley Bridge, Yorkshire in 1890 by Alice Marion Rawson and entered onto the Register of births, deaths and marriages for that year. Had the authorities checked these documents more closely, Alice's claim that she had never had a daughter could have been disproved.

Finally, the 1891 Census records for Bishop Thornton show the presence of a baby by the name of Ida Wiseman Rawson at the home of May Stott, a 55 year-old widow, at Booze Green, Shaw Mills, Bishop Thornton. The child is listed as a 'Nursechild'. This record seems to provide further documentary evidence backing Henry Rawson's statement to the police, that the child was given to another lady to look after.

So, did Alice Parrington kill her illegitimate baby daughter? The timeline is certainly highly suggestive, as were Alice's subsequent actions. Ida vanished either just before, or immediately after, Alice's wedding to Christopher Parrington. The child definitely existed (birth, baptism and census records prove that point), and Alice was legally registered as her mother, of that there is no doubt. We know from her brother's statement that Ida was handed to her mother, who then departed from Ripon Railway Station with her daughter in her arms (as confirmed by her brother), yet no witness or documentation can be found to show that Ida was alive and well at any point after December 1891. Alice's behaviour (changing her name and moving 70 miles from her home in Starbotton after Ida's disappearance) also seems to suggest someone wishing to avoid local gossip and awkward questions.

It seems probable that Alice deliberately denied the existence of Ida, knowing that the decomposed body found in the tin chest was never likely to be identified, therefore creating enough doubt to make any criminal conviction impossible. Today, with the benefit of forensic science and DNA, the child's parentage could be proved almost instantly. Coupled with the very strong and suggestive circumstantial evidence, Alice Parrington would have, almost certainly, been found guilty. Yet, during the Victorian and Edwardian eras, murder convictions were notoriously hard to prove and juries were unwilling to convict on the basis of circumstantial evidence alone. Then, as now, the burden of proof fell on the prosecution to prove 'beyond reasonable doubt' that Alice Parrington had murdered her child. Without the confirmation of the child's identity, that required 'burden of proof' simply could not be achieved. It is always hard for any fair-minded person to believe that a mother could kill her own child, despite the strong circumstantial evidence seeming to point towards the fact. Alice Parrington it seems may have, quite literally, got away with murder. To view the case today, through the lens of history, and with the extra information mentioned here, that evidence seems to be even more compelling and beyond the realms of mere coincidence.

So why were the magistrates at Skipton Town Hall so willing to dismiss the case and set Alice free? Was it (as mentioned earlier) simply too damaging a story for the reputation of the region? The answer may be contained in this extraordinarily vitriolic editorial contained in an edition of the *Leeds Mercury* newspaper from October 1905, in which the correspondent bemoans the effect that the 'Wharfedale Trunk Mystery' was having on the tourist trade:

Wharfedale is, of course, achieving popularity now'-a-days; one has in mind the charming villages of Kettlewell, Starbotton, Buckden and the others which follow each other in even stages to where the Wharf rises. The "Upper Wharfedale Trunk Mystery", as the enterprising sub-editor has described the tragedy which is providing sensation for the peoples of this district, has drawn the public attention to this region of limestone cliffs and breezy moorlands. Unfortunately, for the seeker after peace and quiet, these descriptive writers who have, this season past, worn down their pencils to stumps in extolling—with vocabularies purple with superlatives—the lurid virtues of this poetic landscape. Now, the attractions of the Dales are full to the brim with half-tipsy crowds of holiday hooligans, usually seen at our much-booming seaside watering places, rioting in the streets with mouth organ and concertina. Yet, there are no minstrels here; no pierrots. The Britisher can't enjoy himself here! The sea-side holiday has become an obsession with him and he must stay there. The few who spend a portion of their annual holidays out in our neighbourhood

of stern and wild moorlands may, perhaps, be chagrined at
the thought of their paradise being invaded by the mob. But
with Grassington booming, the moderate privacies of Upper
Wharfedale will become a thing of the past.

Conceivably the leading figures in Wharfedale society were far from pleased with the unwelcome notoriety and lurid headlines that the sordid story of Alice Parrington had brought to the region. Perhaps councillors and business owners alike feared losing their lucrative new trade in well-heeled visitors from London, who were now taking advantage of the railway boom and travelling to spend their leisure time - and money - among the attractive peaks and valleys of the Yorkshire Dales. It appears that the unwelcome publicity attracted by the 'Wharfedale Trunk Mystery' had brought the wrong kind of visitor to the area. Visitors of a lower class, that purchased little and drank much.

Were the magistrates, leading and influential figures in Wharfedale society, only too glad to dismiss the case and thus prevent the region becoming the subject of even more scandalous headlines? It seems a distinct possibility. The case was certainly dismissed with indecent haste, despite continuing speculation among locals. Tellingly, the story did not feature again in the county's press. The needs of Wharfedale society and its business owners, it seems, had superseded justice in the case of eighteen-month old Ida Wiseman Rawson.

What happened to Alice after the sensation and scandal of

the 'Wharfedale Trunk Mystery' became yesterday's news? Her husband Christopher died in 1913, at the age of 50, leaving her a widow with four daughters. He was buried at St Michael's Church in Linton-in-Craven. Alice remarried a man named Joseph Lee at Skipton in 1917 and may have emigrated to the United States shortly afterwards.

THE BROTHER OR THE LOVER?

The sun was beginning to illuminate the sky away to the east as John Marshall made his way along the footpath across the fields between Kirklington and Thornborrow, just a few miles from Ripon. Marshall was a platelayer for the Railway Company, walking to work as he always did. It was precisely a quarter past five in the morning as he reached the hand gate at the point in the barn field next to the mill stream, where the footpath headed west to Thornborrow. As he turned to open the gate he recoiled in shock when he noticed something lying on the ground close to the well-worn footpath. As he approached, he instantly realised it was the body of a young woman.

John Marshall ran as fast as he could towards Kirklington to fetch Police Constable John Hudson. By the time the two men returned to the scene it was almost 5.30am. PC Hudson was an experienced and extremely methodical police officer. He calmly removed his notebook and pencil from his tunic pocket and made the following note (which would later be read in court):

About half-past five o'clock on the morning of Wednesday, the 6th May, 1874, John Marshall came to my house. In consequence of what he told me I returned with him to the barn field, where he had found the dead body of a young woman laid upon the ground, about four yards from the hand- gate leading to Thornbro' and two yards from the footpath. The head was about one and a half feet from the water edge of the mill race. The body was laid straight on its back, with its feet towards the footpath. Her right hand was clenched, with the thumb underneath the fingers, and was raised above the head. The left hand was clenched in the same manner, and was lying by the left side. Her throat was cut and her neckerchief was pushed tight into the cut. The bow and the brooch that were worn at the front being drawn up behind the right ear. No part of the tie was cut. The right side of the face was covered with blood as well as the throat. The lower parts of the skirt of the dress were smeared with blood, and there was a large pool of blood on the footpath about two yards from the feet of the body. There was a little blood also on the grass on the right side of the body. The dress was disordered and thrown above her knees and was torn in two places. In my opinion, death had occurred several hours earlier. I then sent for Dr Mickle, who came to the place before the body had been disturbed.

On the direction of Dr Mickle the body was removed to Mr Horner's public house in Kirklington, as inns were often used as temporary morgues during the Victorian era. Once at the inn, Constable Hudson and Dr Mickle searched the body, removing a love letter, a photograph, a shilling, a hymn book and a pair of kid gloves from the victim's pockets.

PC Hudson then returned to the scene of the crime and continued his search of the nearby field. His efforts were rewarded with the discovery of a woman's umbrella close to the body. During the afternoon he was joined by PC Fothergill and the two officers uncovered a small tobacco pipe, which was stained with blood on both sides of the bowl. As the two men examined the hedge bordering the field, their search yielded part of a broken razor case. Later, a further 700 yards from the crime scene, the other part of the razor case was located. The two parts matched exactly. They also noted a smear of blood on the hand-gate leading out of the field towards Thornborrow.

Meanwhile, the items recovered from the body of the deceased produced two vital pieces of information – the identity of the victim and a possible suspect. The letter contained in young lady's garments was from her fiancé, a 19-year-old local boy named Edwin Gatenby. Addressed to Elizabeth Jackson, the letter, dated the previous day, was a formal rejection of the girl, in which Gatenby had broken off the couple's engagement, also noting that he was returning her photograph. This instantly gave the police the identity and address of the girl and the name of a suspect. Had Elizabeth Jackson refused to break off the engagement, forcing Gatenby to meet her in an isolated spot where he had then killed her? Edwin Gatenby was well known locally as his family lived in the nearby hamlet of Carthorpe. He had entered domestic service at the age of 13 at the home of a wealthy merchant in Bedale, James Barnabas. The police visited the Barnabas' home and arrested Gatenby. However, he was subsequently released as he had been working in the house all day, beginning early in the morning. Three other domestic staff were able to vouch that Gatenby had not left the house during the previous day or two. The police were left without a suspect.

Next, the officers visited the home of the Jacksons in the hamlet of Carthorpe. George Jackson, Elizabeth's father, was a farm labourer but seemed to be comfortably well off, living in a pleasant cottage with his wife and their three children. He had already been out searching for his 16-year-old daughter, when she had not returned that afternoon. Elizabeth had a younger brother, Anthony, aged 12, and an elder brother, William, aged 30. William, it transpired, had left the house early on the Wednesday morning, just fifteen minutes after Elizabeth, and had not been seen since. The police questioned the Jacksons' neighbours, who were able to confirm that William Jackson had argued with his sister during the previous day, telling her, 'You are a fine looking girl, too good for the likes of Edwin Gatenby. He will never have you. I will take care of you!'

William Jackson now seemed to be the strongest suspect in the murder of his sister and the police immediately concentrated their efforts in the hunt for him. It was feared that Jackson may have been looking for a passage to America, in which case it would be almost impossible to locate him.

However, following the death of his sister, William Jackson had headed for Ripon. From there he managed to evade police detection by heading north. On the day following the murder Jackson called at a house in Catterick, to ask for money or food; however, the householders were struck with his odd manner and unusual behaviour and sent him on his way. The next morning, 8th May, he was seen by a witness in Darlington, pawning a waistcoat under a fictitious name. When asked for an address he stated, 'I live anywhere'.

This was followed by a visit to a lady named Mrs Storey (whose evidence would later be heard in court). Jackson was next seen heading towards Bishop Auckland.

Whilst heading in the direction of the town he noticed a policeman, walking towards him. The sight of the police officer caused Jackson to panic and he turned and ran into a nearby colliery yard. PC Wright chased after him, blowing his whistle to attract the attention of other officers, who joined in the search. Despite Jackson's efforts to hide among the coal wagons, he was soon captured and arrested. He was then transferred to Wath Police Station and held in a cell overnight to await a magistrates hearing the following morning.

William Jackson almost evaded justice again, this time by attempting to take his own life. Whilst waiting in his prison cell he endeavoured to slit his own throat, using a piece of sharpened tin. Some of his food had been brought to his cell in a tin can. It appears that Jackson had broken a piece from the tin can and somehow managed to sharpen it against the cell wall. Fortunately, he was discovered in time. The police surgeon managed to staunch the flow of blood and Jackson was declared fit and able to face a magistrates' hearing.

Despite Jackson's unusual and detached behaviour at his initial magistrates' arraignment, it was nevertheless decided that he was fit to face trial for the murder of his sister and a date was set for Friday 31st July 1874 at the Crown Court in York.

The trial was remarkable for two reasons. Firstly, the hearing was spread across two days (an almost unheard-of event in the Victorian era, when the majority of trials were completed within one day). Secondly, Prime Minister Benjamin Disraeli took a personal interest in the case; having followed the hunt for William Jackson in the newspapers.

Proceedings were opened by Mr Justice Denham, Mr. Price, QC, and Mr Whitaker appeared for the prosecution. Initially Jackson refused any defence representation; however, he was persuaded by Mr Justice Denham that his case would best be served with a legal defence. It is worth remembering that a defendant was not able to speak in his own defence in a British Court of Law until 1898, as it was feared that they would generally prejudice their own case. Mr Etherington Smith was hastily appointed to defend

Jackson and the case was able to begin in front of a packed public gallery.

The prosecution began their case by calling William Jackson's father to testify as a witness against his own son.

George Jackson was asked to detail his son's circumstances and background to the court. William Jackson, his father explained:

He had been a private in the 77th Regiment for nine years, during which time he had served in India. Latterly, after being discharged, William returned to England, and entered the reserve force. He had lived several weeks with us up to May. and had drank heavily and caused many domestic quarrels. On the night before the murder, we had quarrelled. And I had threatened to send for a constable. William said: 'if one came, blood would be shed. Half of these murders are committed by aggravating a man when he is drunk!

I replied, *Murderers are always caught when they have done it.* to which William answered menacingly, *I'll watch any one from catching me!*

Despite the argument and the tense atmosphere within the household, William had stayed in the house until later that afternoon. He then packed up his knapsack to leave home. Meanwhile, his sister, Elizabeth, informed her mother that she had business to attend to in Ripon and left the house in the late afternoon. She appeared to be in good spirits and it was remarked upon by Mr Justice Denham that, 'the prisoner says he thought more about Elizabeth than all the rest of the family.'

Shortly after Elizabeth left home, William also left, telling his family he was heading to Ripon too, to search for work as a 'wood-leader' (someone who led a horse and cart carrying timber). At some point during his walk across the fields he caught up with his sister, as two witnesses noticed the pair walking together. The first witness, a farm servant named John Clarke, recalled seeing William Jackson and his sister walking towards Kirklington on the evening of the 5th May. Clarke even asked Jackson where he was going, to which he received the cryptic response, 'Ripon, if we land'. A second witness, a farmer called John Wells, remembered seeing William and Elizabeth Jackson walking through the Barn Field around 7pm that evening. Crucially, he remembered that Jackson was smoking a short clay pipe; similar to the bloodstained pipe found at the scene. This strong eyewitness sighting may have been enough to convict Jackson there and then, but the prosecution did not rest.

Dr Mickle confirmed to the court the full extent of the injuries suffered by the victim. He also stated for that record, that, in his opinion, Elizabeth Jackson could not have inflicted the injuries upon herself, proven by the fact that she could not then have disposed of the murder weapon at the point it was found, over 700 yards away . The doctor also confirmed that he 'had found the existence of bloodstains on the prisoner's clothing, but cannot say whether they were human.'

The final witness called by the Crown was, perhaps, the most bizarre. Mary Storey, the wife of an innkeeper, recounted for the court a surreal conversation that had taken place between herself and the accused on the day following the murder. Jackson had called into the Storey's inn in Walworth, Durham, on his escape north the day after his sister's death. He took tea with Mrs Storey and proceeded to tell her the story of his sister's murder in the third person, relating the events through the eyes of another imaginary brother,

'I have a sister to bury tomorrow Mrs Storey; her brother has murdered her.'

Mrs Storey enquired, 'Why did he murder her?'

'The only thing I know was that the girl was going with a young man against the will of her brother. Poor thing, I have seen her; she looked black about the mouth, but the other part of her face was as white as snow. She was sixteen years of age, but anyone would take her for twenty, and she was a fine-looking girl'.

Mrs Storey replied, 'The brother must be a villain', to which Jackson answered, 'the brother who has murdered her was a soldier and had been in the Indies. I think he has gone to America, and will never be heard of again'.

Before the defence was called, an assessment of Jackson's mental state was presented to the court. Firstly, a former colleague from the 77th Regiment informed the court that Jackson, while in the Army, 'had received a severe blow on the head, from which he was over five weeks in the hospital. He afterwards complained of his head, saying that if he got any drink in him, it flew to his head and then he was ruined. He had also suffered sunstroke while in India and never fully recovered from it.'

A medical examination of William Jackson by Dr Anderson, undertaken during Jackson's period in remand at Armley Jail in Leeds, reported the following to the court:

I would consider that the murder of a near relative, without absence of motive, would lead me to believe that the case was one of homicidal mania, but the absence of motive must be clearly established. If there were no quarrel or estrangement of any kind then I should be inclined to attribute the crime to an act of homicidal mania. I have especially observed the prisoner, who has been under my care, and I have observed no symptoms of insanity about him.

Next came the case for the defence, carried out by the hastily appointed Mr Etherington Smith. Sadly, it appears the defence for William Jackson may have been one of the weakest ever presented in a British murder trial. Not a single witness was called by the defence. Nor was a plea for insanity filed with the court, despite Jackson's unhinged behaviour and strange demeanour throughout the proceeding. Instead, Mr Etherington Smith spoke for just a few minutes, pleading to the jury for mercy:

I contend that the blow on the head which the prisoner received in the Army unhinged him, and after that all who had intimate connection with him noticed the change that had come over him. I would not attempt to deny that the girl had died at the hands of the prisoner, but I urge that the love he bore for her, and the total absence of motive, all showed that he could not have killed her maliciously, but that he had done the deed under an uncontrollable impulse for which he was not responsible.

Mr Justice Denham, who summed up at great length, expressed the opinion that 'if the wide notion of homicidal mania is that a man in a sudden mad impulse was to not be responsible for the deed he had committed, then the lives of people would not be held anything so dear as they now are'.

The jury required just a short deliberation, returning to the court room in a matter of minutes with a verdict of 'Guilty of wilful murder'. Mr Justice Denham solemnly passed sentence on William Jackson:

You had been found guilty of wilful murder. If the jury had hesitated long in finding you guilty, then I would have considered that the lives of your fellow- creatures would not be safe, as the law intended and desired to make it so. That you, the prisoner, have put your sister out of this world with a determined purpose - from what internal motive no one knows - no person who has heard this trial could for a moment doubt. It is now my duty to pass the sentence of the law upon you.

William Jackson was sentenced to death and led from the court to be returned to jail, where he would await his sentence. No clemency was granted and Jackson was hanged for the murder of his sister at York Castle on 18th August 1874.

Was William Jackson guilty of his sister's murder? On
the balance of probability, yes. Did he receive a fair trial?
Almost certainly not. The testimony against him was
largely circumstantial. There were no witnesses to the
actual crime, nor any evidence that directly linked him to
the murder. Nor was any motive every discovered for the
attack on his sister. While it is not essential under English
Law to establish a motive in the crime of murder; the
absence of one usually offers some 'reasonable doubt',
as did the presence of another equally credible suspect,
Edwin Gatenby. The lack of a proper defence, coupled
with the accused's state of mind (who was surely, by
legal definition, insane at the time of the killing), were
clearly grounds for a degree of mercy in the sentencing.
Mitigating circumstances such as drunkenness, often being
taken into account by Victorian juries, to an extent that
could not be conceived of today.

It must also be remembered, that with the absence
of eyewitnesses, forensic or scientific evidence,
verdicts were often made based on three deciding
factors – circumstantial evidence, character, and
previous behaviour. William Jackson, it seems, was an
unsympathetic defendant who was unable, or unwilling,
to sway the jury in his favour. Tragically for Jackson, the
Court of Appeal, giving a defendant the right to legally
appeal his verdict, was established just one year later.

FEWSTON – THE SHOTGUN
AND THE SHOVEL

Robert William Moore was described by those who knew
him as a likeable young man. While still a child in 1933,
he had moved to Yorkshire from Canada with his mother.
After a brief spell in the Army, following the war, he
had turned his hand to taxi driving; and from there to
secondhand car sales. He had married in 1950 and moved
into a small house in Harlow Avenue in Harrogate. Before
long the couple had their first son. It was now May 1953.
Britain was emerging from a harsh and cruel winter. The
North Sea Floods had devastated large parts of Britain's
east coast, Queen Mary had died, and the public was
horrified at the discovery of the six bodies at 10 Rillington
Place in London, where it became clear that a catastrophic
miscarriage of justice had taken place. However, despite his
protests, there was to be no such miscarriage of justice in
the case of Robert William Moore.

Earlier that month, Robert Moore had purchased a used
motor car from a fellow car dealer and acquaintance,
Edward Watson from the Shadwell area of Leeds. Moore
had paid Edward Watson £55 for the car (approximately

£1,500 today). However, on returning home with the car, Moore discovered that the chassis was cracked and there was some hidden corrosion. Moore was furious with Watson, who refused to refund his money. Instead, Watson taunted Moore telling him, 'it's your pigeon now!'

Robert Moore then spent a sizeable amount of money repairing the car's chassis and attempted to sell it via the Motor Auctions in Leeds. However, he was unable to achieve his reserve price at the auction. In a later statement to the police Moore would accuse Edward Watson of deliberately driving the price of the car down at the sales, so as to sabotage his attempts to retrieve his outlay. 'Every time I put it in the car sales, Watson cribbed it and started it at a low price,' Moore explained, 'I was stuck with the car for about a fortnight. I had to repair the chassis at a cost of £6 and I eventually managed to sell it for £40.'

Robert Moore brooded silently and determined to seek his revenge on Edward Watson.

Shortly afterwards, on 30th May 1953, Moore invited Watson to accompany him to Harrogate to view a 'Shooting Brake' (what would now be called an estate car) that was for sale. Surprisingly, considering their recent fall out, Watson agreed, and the pair set out from Leeds. In a later statement, allegedly made by Moore, he told police officers that, 'we reached Beckwithshaw. I had the full intention of taking him into the woods and clouting him.' Fortunately for Edward Watson, the car ran out of petrol and too much time was lost. Watson told Moore that he needed to return to Leeds; and Moore's opportunity to seek his revenge had passed. He had no intention of waiting, however, and the following day he arranged to meet Watson once more.

When morning arrived, Sunday 31st May, Edward Watson rose early and left his home in Leeds, telling his wife Anita that he was going to meet Robert Moore at 10am with the intention of journeying to Harrogate to buy a car. He took a substantial amount of money with him, in cash, probably in the region of £100 - £150 (around £3,000 today).

Meanwhile Robert Moore had been busy. Through a contact, William Metcalfe, he purchased a Winchester .22 rifle, some cartridges, and a silencer. Moore explained that the firearm was for shooting pheasants. He put the rifle in the boot of the car, together with a spade.

By nightfall that Sunday, when Edward Watson had still not returned, his wife Anita began to worry. She waited and waited. Eventually she retired to bed, hoping her husband would return while she was asleep. When she woke the following morning and he was still not home she decided to wait a little longer, in case he had decided to stay the night in Harrogate. The day passed and there was still no word. After a fraught and worried night, in which she hardly slept, she decided to ask her Uncle, Lewis Howe, to accompany her to call on Robert Moore and see if he could shed light on her husband's disappearance. Mr Howe and Anita Watson called on Moore and asked if he could help them trace her husband's whereabouts. Moore told them he was unable to help. He explained that he had made an appointment with Watson for 10am on the morning of 31st May, but Watson had not turned up. He had waited 15 minutes, then left. Howe asked him if he bore any grievance against Watson. Moore admitted that he did. After recounting the story of the car with the damaged chassis to Howe, Moore seemed both agitated and afraid. He then followed Lewis Howe and Anita Watson back to their car and, as they left, promised that 'if I hear anything, I will let you know straight away'. They both noted that Moore appeared to be 'all of a tremble'.

The pair both felt uncomfortable with Moore's manner and demeanour and decided to pass their suspicions on to the police. They reported the matter, explaining their concerns and the facts regarding the ongoing vendetta between Moore and Watson. It was enough grounds for suspicion and Detective Sergeant Harry Wilby decided to pay a house call on Robert Moore. He interviewed Moore under caution, expecting a cagey response. However, when Sergeant Wilby asked Moore if he 'knew anything about the whereabouts of Edward Watson', he could not possibly have anticipated the answer he would receive. A visibly nervous and pale Moore replied jokingly, 'Why? You don't think I have shot and buried him, do you?" Sergeant Wilby left and returned to the police station with some serious doubts playing on his mind. Moore had seemed visibly nervous and jumpy during the brief interview. He decided to investigate the matter further. Inquiries revealed that Moore had purchased a .22 rifle, using his Aunt's residence in Killinghall, just north of Harrogate, as the registered location of the firearm. Sergeant Wilby set off to recover the weapon. However, an unexpected development in the case forced Sergeant Wilby to turn his car around and return to Harrogate.

The police were notified by Harrogate District Hospital that Robert Moore had attempted to take his own life immediately after the police officers had left his house. He had been rushed to hospital as a result of his failed suicide bid. Seemingly, directly after Sergeant Wilby's departure, earlier that day, Moore had attempted to take his own life by inhaling the supply of coal gas into the kitchen. He had first sealed the doors and windows to the room airtight. Fortunately, he was discovered, slumped on the floor, by a neighbour. Coal gas (or Town Gas as it was sometimes called) was produced by the high temperature burning of coal and was piped into homes linked to the coal gas grid. Sadly, coal gas was highly dangerous; containing up to 20% carbon monoxide. By the 1950s it was Britain's most common method of suicide (by the early 1970s, it had been replaced by the recently discovered natural gas, which contains little or no carbon monoxide).

In a state of panic Robert Moore had tried to poison himself by breathing in the noxious gas. However, he had panicked and aborted the attempt, leaving himself coughing, gasping and in a state of semi-consciousness. He was admitted to Harrogate District Hospital for treatment. Convinced the suicide attempt was an admission of guilt, a police officer was placed next to Moore's bed, should he attempt to flee upon regaining consciousness.

When Moore's faculties returned, he woke to find Sergeant Wilby at his bedside. The time was 11.50pm and five days has passed since Edward Watson's disappearance. As Moore looked up, Sergeant Wilby said to him, 'Now then Bob, let's have the truth. It will be better for you.'

Moore, seemingly relieved, blurted out, 'I told Watson I knew where there was a car for sale in Harrogate and we should see It. On the way in the car I told him to pull up, I had seen a pheasant and told him I wanted to shoot it. I had a gun with me. I got out of the car and shot him. This was at Fewston. I panicked a bit and carried him over the wall into the wood, and then dug a three--foot trench and put him in it. He was dead. I covered him over. I shot at him and not at a pheasant. When I was putting him in the hole I felt money in his pockets, which I took, thinking I might need it to leave the country. I took about hundred and some pounds out of his pocket. I put the gun and spade at my mother's house in a cellar under the stairs.'

At this stage, however, the statement had not been made under formal caution, nor in the presence of a solicitor. Its admissibility as evidence in a court of law would later become a matter for debate.

Moore was immediately arrested and escorted to
Harrogate Police Station (despite having regained
consciousness from his suicide attempt less than an
hour earlier). He was questioned by Sergeant Wilby and
Inspector Winter.

The Sergeant warned Moore, 'Do you fully realise what you
are saying?'

Moore nodded and informed the police officers that 'I
shot Watson and buried him at Fewston, in a wood near
a reservoir. I am prepared to show you where. We can tell
the place because I knocked some stones off the top of the
wall when I lifted him over it.'

It was now 12.25am at night. Despite the lateness of the
hour the police did not wish to waste any time. Armed with
flashlights, the officers escorted Robert Moore to Fewston.
After crossing the Reservoir Bridge, Moore instructed
Sergeant Wilby to slow the car down. On reaching
Primrose Cottage Plantation, Moore pointed in the
direction of a low stone wall with a small spinney beyond
it. 'It is over there', he announced, leading the officers over
the wall and through the trees, 'We'll have a job to find

it, because I covered it with twigs to make it look natural. There is some clay on a tree where I wiped my spade.'

By torchlight Sergeant Wilby was able to find the tree, which also had a distinctive V shape cut into the bark. On locating the tree, Moore instantly recognised the spot and pointed to a patch of ground, 'The body is there!'. The police officers began to dig and soon located the body of Edward Watson in a shallow grave, approximately 3 feet deep. His body was face down in a kneeling position, having been shot five times at close range.

The story, which had gripped the public's attention in Yorkshire, became a national front-page story. Following consultation with the Director of Public Prosecutions, 16th July was fixed as the date for the initial arraignment at Otley Magistrates' Court. Mr E Wurzal was appointed as Moore's solicitor. Importantly, it was ruled at the hearing that Moore's original statement, given at hospital and at the police station, could be read in court and would be admissible as evidence. Moore was formerly charged on two accounts, one count of murder, and one of attempted suicide (still an offence in 1953). Moore pleaded 'not guilty' and a trial date was set for 23rd November at Leeds Assizes.

The trial began, in front of a packed public gallery. Moore entered a plea of 'not guilty' and the case for the prosecution began. A series of witnesses, including Edward Watson's wife, recounted their suspicions regarding Moore's behaviour. His statement to the police made in June was read out to the court and Mr G Raymond Hinchcliffe, appearing for the Crown, intimated to the jury that Moore's grievance against Edward Watson had been the motive behind the shooting. It was also suggested by Mr Hinchcliffe that Moore had seen Watson in possession of a large amount of cash at the previous day's car auctions, and that robbery was another possible motive. A further witness (Robert Moore's aunt) was able to confirm that she had lent him £375 in 1952, thus confirming that he was blighted by money problems.

A further witness, William Metcalfe, an associate of Moore's, was also able to confirm selling a .22 rifle to him on the day prior to the shooting.

In his defence Robert Moore claimed that the shooting was accidental. He asserted that he and Edward Watson had gone pheasant shooting together, and that Watson had grabbed the gun barrel which had then accidentally discharged. Moore then claimed that Watson had cried out 'you have caught me' and that 'Watson then started pulling on the barrel which went off three or four times.' Only then, in panic, did he decide to bury Watson's body for fear of being blamed.

The fact that Moore had already offered two different explanations since the day of the tragedy, followed by a last-minute story claiming that the shooting was accidental, did not carry any weight with the jury.

In summing up Mr Justice Stable was patently unimpressed with Moore's version of events. The fact that Moore had taken a shovel with him on that fateful day clearly indicated pre-meditation. He instructed the jury that

'the question of manslaughter does not arise. There is
no halfway house in this case. The verdict must be either
murder or accidental death, if you believe these three
police officers' evidence, it completely negates Moore's
story of the accident.'

Mr Justice Stable also pointed out that if the shooting had
genuinely been an accident, 'why on earth did he not say
so then? Why did he put his signature to a statement in
which he says, "I shot him"?'

The jury retired for one hour and forty minutes to
consider its verdict, before returning with a unanimous
verdict of 'guilty'. One of the female jury members wept
openly as Mr Justice Stable donned his black cap and
pronounced the death penalty, 'Robert William Moore,
the jury has returned a verdict of guilty on the clearest
possible evidence.' Throughout the pronouncement
Moore remained calm and composed, staring intently
at the judge, his eyes unmoved. Moore's barrister, Mr
Rudolph Lyons Q.C informed the court of their immediate
intention to file an appeal.

There was to be no overturning of the conviction on
appeal, however. Lord Goddard, the Lord Chief Justice,
turned down Moore's appeal on 18th December, describing
it as 'a sheer waste of time. Moore had been guilty of a
cruel and deliberate murder'. A petition for clemency,
containing thousands of signatures, was organised
immediately and presented to the Home Secretary, but this
too failed. A date for the execution was fixed.

Robert Moore was hanged at Armley prison in Leeds on Tuesday the 5th January 1954, by Public Executioner Steven Wade. A notice confirming the execution was posted on the prison gates for the handful of reporters that had gathered outside. The Governor and Medical Officer of the prison confirmed that the execution had been 'carried out in an expeditious and proper manner'. Moore was then buried without ceremony at the prison cemetery at Armley. He was not yet 27 years old.

Edward Watson, only one year older than Robert Moore at the time of his murder, was buried in a quiet, family ceremony. Two weeks after the execution of Moore, Edward Watson's widow, Anita, received £120 compensation from Otley Magistrates' Court, following the sale of Moore's saloon car and rifle. The money stolen from her husband's pocket on the day of the murder was also returned to her.

"I WILL KILL SOMEONE"

There can be few more beautiful and serene sites, amongst the rugged splendour of the Yorkshire Dales, than the manicured and tranquil grounds of Studley Park, nestled in the eastern Dales, close to Ripon. Yet the grounds of the Studley Park Estate, containing the stately Fountains Hall and the monastic ruins of Fountains Abbey, were the setting for the darkest of tragedies on a pleasant summer's evening in June 1917.

The Great War was at its height. The American army had recently joined the conflict, yet the vast opposing armies were still deadlocked. The Battle of Messines Ridge in Belgium had just commenced. On 7th June 1917, in an extraordinary endeavour by Allied tunnelling teams, 455 tons of high explosive was detonated underneath the Messines Ridge, a stronghold of the German forces. Along with the entire town of Messines, 10,000 German soldiers were killed. It was the largest non-nuclear explosion in the history of mankind, and was heard as far away as London, York, and even Dublin.

Many men from the Yorkshire Regiments were away fighting in the fields of France and Belgium and the Yorkshire newspapers carried a seemingly endless list of casualties or 'MIAs' (Missing In Action). For some soldiers, not classified fit enough for the front line, the barracks at Ripon must have felt a safe and fortunate posting. Two such men were Arthur Peacock and Charles John Yates. Both men had volunteered in 1915 and joined the 3rd Battalion, Royal Field Artillery, Yorkshire Regiment. Classified 'not fit for front line duty' they were assigned catering and driving duties with their battery; then stationed at the Ripon Barracks. The two men become close, and their friendship lasted throughout enlistment and basic training.

Arthur Peacock hailed from Stockton in Durham. His father had been employed in the Tyne shipyards as a clerk and Arthur had been raised in a happy home, along with his two brothers and two sisters until he was about 10 years of age. At that time, his father had been committed to a lunatic asylum, in which he sadly died shortly afterwards. This left the family without means and the children were all forced to venture out and seek work, in an effort to support their mother, Hannah Peacock. Indeed, the 1901 and 1911 census both comment simply, 'Hannah Peacock, Widow, no means'. Arthur managed to find work first as a coachbuilder's apprentice, and subsequently at a large blacksmith's forge (perhaps through his elder brother, who had already begun work there).

At the age of 18 Arthur married his childhood sweetheart,

Martha, who moved into Arthur's family home in Brunswick Street, Stockton-on-Tees. The couple raised five children of their own and, although money was tight, the couple seemed to be happy. Soon afterwards, however, Arthur developed health problems which resulted in him being dismissed from his job at the blacksmith's forge. From that point onwards, it seems, he struggled to find regular employment.

In September 1915, then aged 38, he enlisted with the Royal Field Artillery in Middlesbrough. The army, by the end of 1915, had a severe manpower shortage as they simply could not recruit quickly enough to match the rate at which soldiers were being lost on the front lines. Despite this urgent requirement, Arthur's medical examination discovered that he was suffering from a valvular disease of the heart and it was noted on his army record that he should be 'Classified C2 – suitable for light duties only'. He was then posted to the barracks at Ripon, initially as a waiter in the Officers' Mess, then as a driver.

Charles Yates, who had been born in a quiet Warwickshire village, was 21 when he had enlisted, along with Arthur Peacock, in 1915. Now 23 years of age and despite the fact that Peacock was 15 years his senior, the men had become the firmest of friends.

On the morning of Monday 11th June 1917, Arthur Peacock complained of a headache and tried to walk around with his eyes closed. When he did so, he staggered alarmingly. A request to attend sick parade in the medical block was granted; and he was seen by the medical officer, Lieutenant

Morgan. Peacock explained his unsettling symptoms to the officer, who diagnosed some form of 'brain incoordination' (an affliction of the part of the brain dealing with balance and movement). Lieutenant Morgan arranged to see Peacock again later that evening, then advised him to return to his quarters and rest. Peacock did so, and lay on his bed for the remainder of the morning, still complaining of horrendous, blinding pains in his head. At about 1pm he rose from his bed and went to ask his friend Private Charles Yates (known as Charlie by his colleagues) if he could borrow a razor. However, when he entered the hut in which Charlie slept the room was empty. He searched for a razor but was unable to find one, so left. He managed to locate Charlie and a few moments later the two men returned to Charlie's billet, whereupon Charlie was seen handing a razor to him. The men seemed on friendly terms.

As the afternoon was warm and sunny the two men decided to go for a walk across the fields into Mackershaw Wood, on the Studley Park Estate. Much of the estate had been commandeered by the army during the war and was being used for a variety for training exercises, supply dumps and drills. It would have been likely that they passed several other soldiers during their walk.

Around 4pm the Military Guard on duty at the camp entrance noticed Arthur Peacock walking back alone, coming from the direction of Mackershaw Wood. As he approached the gates the guard asked him, 'Where's Charlie?' Arthur replied, 'I want to go to the guard room'.

He was escorted inside the guard room. Once inside, he walked up to the Sergeant's desk and, without emotion, said, 'I have come to give myself up, as I have cut a man's throat with his razor.' (Before the introduction of the safety razor lessened the availability of cut-throat razors to the general public, the cut-throat variety was the weapon of choice in a simply staggering number of murders, vicious attacks and suicides each year). Peacock produced a blood-stained cut-throat razor from his pocket and handed it to the sergeant. As he was led away he turned and added, 'you will find him on the path in the field that leads to the bombing range.'

Arthur Peacock was immediately placed under arrest by the duty sergeant. As he was led away to a cell, the sergeant enquired, 'Why did you do it?'. Peacock casually remarked, 'There was no malice. I had no cause to do it; something just came over me and told me to do it, and so I did it.'

The military police contacted the civil police in Ripon, as the crime had taken place outside of the army camp, and officers were despatched to Studley Park, with their efforts to be concentrated on the area known as Mackershaw Wood. The officers, led by Inspector Blacker from Ripon police station, were soon at the scene, taking advantage of the long summer evenings to search the area. It did not take them long to find the body of Charlie Yates, just as Peacock had told them, by the footpath in the field just outside Mackershaw Wood. He was lying on his back in the

grass, his head bent back at a hideous and unnatural angle
from his shoulders. His throat had been sliced from ear to
ear. So savage and deep was the wound, it had penetrated
right through to the bone. The sight was truly shocking.
One of the police officers later reported that, 'the head
was practically severed from the body. You would not think
an implement as small as a razor could cause so deep a
wound.'

Police officers immediately removed Arthur Peacock from
military detention at Ripon Barracks and formerly arrested
him. When charged, he again repeated, 'there was no
malice in it'. Peacock was then remanded at Armley Jail in
Leeds for a period of seven days, to allow an inquiry into
the circumstances of the brutal killing to take place. After
this initial period of investigation, the decision was made
to formally charge Arthur Peacock with murder on the
27th June 1917, with a court date set for Thursday 19th July
at the Yorkshire Assizes in Leeds.

The trial was a rather sombre affair, not attracting the
crowds usually associated with high profile murder cases.
It seemed that the population of Leeds was rather jaded
at the thought of, and perhaps unable to stomach, yet
another tragic story to emerge from the war. If any proof
were needed of the public's failing appetite for yet more
stories of tragedy and loss, the *Yorkshire Post* - on an almost
daily basis – published the 'short' and the 'long' lists
of casualties from the front line. In the week preceding
Arthur Peacock's trial, the Post announced the following
casualty lists taken from the West Yorkshire and Duke of
Wellington Regiments alone – 'Killed 57, Wounded 193,

Missing (Presumed Dead) 1,080 Total 1,330'.

Arthur Peacock appeared in court in uniform and wearing his horn-rimmed spectacles. Mr Justice McCardie enquired, 'How do you plead?'. 'Not guilty, my Lord', came the reply.

First to give evidence at Peacock's trial was Lieutenant Morgan, RAMC, who had examined the prisoner on the morning before the death of Charlie Yates. Lieutenant Morgan confirmed that Peacock had been suffering from headaches and problems with his balance, which the doctor had put down to 'brain incoordination'. Later that evening, Lieutenant Morgan confirmed, he had been asked to re-examine Peacock in his prison cell, following his arrest, 'I again examined his eyes. They were suffused, and somewhat bloodshot, and his answers to me were confused.'

Mr Richard Luck KC, led for the prosecution stating that, 'the affair was a painful tragedy in which the facts were undisputed. The man whose life the prisoner took was a friend of his, and the only question which faces the jury would be that of the prisoner's state of mind at the time of committing the act.' The prosecution asserted that there had been no previous signs of any mental illness in Arthur Peacock, nor anything in his behaviour that would have suggested the shocking events of 11th July. Mr EFL Mortimer would refute this suggestion during their presentation for the defence.

The prosecution rested and Mr Mortimer began the case for Peacock's defence. That Arthur Peacock had killed

Private Yates was never disputed; the defence rested purely on Peacock's state of mind at the time. Fellow soldiers from Ripon Camp attested to the great friendship between the two men, 'they were almost inseparable, always took their walks together, they never had a quarrel, and there were no grounds for quarrel'. Several other soldiers at the Ripon Camp testified to previously 'noticing that there was something wrong in the mind of Peacock.' The defence claimed that Peacock was regularly depressed and morose. He had, apparently, complained on frequent occasions of severe pains in his head. In fact, several years before joining the army, he had been forced to give up work at the blacksmith's forge, where he had been employed, due to severe headaches and dizziness.

A fellow soldier, Private Thomas, alleged that Peacock had made an unprovoked attack on him some years previously. However, he had not wanted to press charges at the time, for fear of getting another soldier into trouble. Private Thomas had also warned Private Yates, on the morning of his death, not to go for his usual walk with Peacock, as he feared that Peacock might attack him. Unfortunately, Yates had chosen to disregard his advice. To offer such a piece of advice strongly suggests that Arthur Peacock's colleagues were already concerned about his potential behaviour.

Further medical evidence was presented to the court by the defence. Dr Exley, the medical officer at Armley Jail, expressed the opinion that Peacock was insane at the time he had committed the offence. Peacock's suicidal tendencies were also presented; upon which Mr Justice

McCardie sought some clarification,

Doctor, do you think that, because he asked for the razor beforehand, he intended to commit suicide?'

'I do, your Honour, 'I think there is evidence of that tendency in his character'.

'Dr Exley, would not the theory that he killed Yates in order that he might be shot himself, be consistent with the facts?'

'No', replied Dr Exley, 'because I do not think he formed an intention to kill Yates sufficiently long beforehand.'

'And, doctor, is it your opinion that he did not think it morally wrong to kill Private Yates?'

'That is so'.

Unsurprisingly, given the weight of medical and circumstantial evidence, the jury found that Arthur Peacock was 'guilty, but that he was insane at the time of committing the act.' Mr Justice McCardie ordered that Arthur Peacock, 'should be detained at a secure institution during His Majesty's pleasure.'
He was removed from the court and transferred to a high security mental hospital, where he would spend the rest of his days. His wife, Martha, remained in Stockton-on-Tees to look after the couple's five children, the eldest of whom was 15, the youngest just 6. Tragically,

Martha died just 15 months later in October 1918, aged just 38 (possibly during the Spanish Flu epidemic, which was felt particularly acutely in the north of England). The five children were effectively orphaned.

Private Yates, who perhaps thought he would sit out the Great War in the relative safety of Ripon, was granted an official Commonwealth War Grave and buried at St Swithin's Church in the quiet village of Lower Quinton, Warwickshire, close to his family home. He was only 23 years old at the time of his death.

If any further proof were needed in such a tragic case, during a subsequent search of Peacock's personal effects, the following letter was found. Addressed by Peacock to his commanding officer, it had been placed in an envelope but never delivered:

TO THE OFFICER COMMANDING THE 1st RESERVE BRIGADE, LEFT SECTION, RIPON

Sir,

I would be grateful if you would give orders for me to be shot out of my misery. I cannot stand the pain in my head any longer. My father died in a lunatic asylum through a softening of the brain, and for a bit now I have been out of my head with the pains in it.

I think it would be a great favour for me if you would have me shot, and no one would be any the wiser. I will kill someone, if you do not, or commit suicide. For I feel as if I cannot help myself,

Private Arthur Peacock.

THE HARROGATE JEWEL ROBBERIES

The pleasant town of Harrogate, on the eastern fringes of the Yorkshire Dales, grew in popularity and wealth from the 18th century onwards, thanks to the discovery of spring waters. Gradually, the town attracted increasing numbers of affluent visitors, all keen to sample the life-preserving properties of the waters. Soon, a succession of hotels, jewellery shops, theatres, and restaurants were built, to cater for the new, and wealthy, arrivals. Unfortunately, by the middle of the Victorian era, the town had become a magnet for the county's most sophisticated, brazen and daring jewel thieves. Harrogate was to develop into the jewellery theft capital of Europe, with the police always seemingly one step behind. By the 1920s, the summer season was referred to by the local police as simply 'the jewel robbery season'.

The ingenuity and bravado of a succession of light-fingered felons was breath-taking and worthy of any Hollywood heist movie.

A daring burglary in 1835, in which a close friend of Queen Victoria's, The Duchess of Gordon, was relieved of £10,000 worth of jewellery, caused a nationwide sensation. The cool thieves removed the jewellery without leaving a single clue or even a hint that the room had been burgled. The theft, worth today's equivalent of more than £1 million, had three noteworthy side effects. Firstly, it educated the criminal underclass that jewellery heists offered huge rewards, balanced against very little risk. Secondly, it caused wealthy and terrified Victorian ladies to create cunning hiding places within their homes. Thirdly, when these ladies then chose to travel to towns such as Harrogate, to sample the spa waters, they no longer wished to leave their jewellery and gems at home. Instead, the hotel rooms and jewellery shops of Harrogate became the thieves' number one target.

Initially, their efforts were crude. A robbery at Harrogate's oldest jewellers, Antonio Fattorini's, in Regent's Parade during July 1871 was a typical early and poorly planned example of the criminal gangs' efforts. The thieves prised away the window bars and ripped down three wooden shutters. They then smashed a large square of plate glass and removed a window display tray containing £100 worth of rings and brooches (worth approximately £11,000 today). The empty tray was later found in a garden. All the articles bore a private hallmark and were instantly recognisable. The burglars were apprehended the very next day, attempting to sell the easily identifiable goods.

They would learn quickly, however, and their efforts would soon become ever more ingenious and audacious. A new standard in boldness was set between 1874 and 1877 by one

William George, who committed a series of daring hotel robberies across the country. He applied a new, and highly successful tactic which would become the modus operandi for most of the future hotel robberies in the town.

Dressed as a well-to-do and respectable businessman, he checked into the Beech Wood Hotel in Harrogate. He then began to systematically ingratiate himself with the other summer residents in the hotel's restaurant, keeping a watchful eye on the ladies' jewellery and on their comings and goings. Within a matter of days, several valuable antiques and items of jewellery vanished from guests' bedrooms. Unfortunately for William George, his attempts to pawn the goods raised the suspicions of the police and he was arrested by Inspector Stott of the Harrogate police. Hanging on the bedroom door of his room at the Beech Wood Hotel was an ingeniously designed waistcoat, which concealed a hidden pocket, inside of which was £13 stolen from the bedroom of a wealthy guest, Mrs Nutter of London. Hidden in the room the police also found most of the proceeds of William George's series of robberies across the country, jewellery worth £300 (£35,000 today), plus a jemmy, a large number of keys and lock picking equipment, and a series of disguises. The thieves were becoming more sophisticated.

Described in court as 'a gentlemanly looking person, 40 years of age, and dressed as a draper', William George was sentenced to 10 years' hard labour at Wakefield Courthouse.

However, William George's stint in prison did not reduce the number of robberies in Harrogate. Two clever thieves, Fulton and Watson, removed substantial amounts of jewellery from guests at the Harrogate Hydro in 1880. Using the proceeds from the thefts, the pair fled to the continent. Their names, although not well known at the time, would soon become internationally famous after they masterminded a daring robbery of the wealthy Madame Chauvet on the Rue des Capucines, Paris, during 1881. With one robber disguised as a colonel and the other impersonating a woman, the pair pulled a 'distraction and switch' routine on the affluent Madame Chauvet. The robbery caused a sensation and the jewel thieves of England descended on Harrogate to attempt their own versions of the spectacular crime.

In 1882 Mr Seymour, a guest staying at the Prospect Hotel in Harrogate, was stopped in the hotel corridor by four burly men, as he returned to his room. Claiming to be police officers, the men informed him that his hotel room had been robbed while he had been out on business. They accompanied him back to his room and duly checked his valuables to find that nothing was missing. The men apologised for the mistake and left. The following day, while Mr Seymour was out for the day, his room was systemically stripped clean – the thieves knew exactly where to look. Following the robbery Mr Seymour sued a waiter at the hotel, claiming that he was involved, and that 'this sort of thing never happens at the Queen's Hotel!'. He lost the case and was forced to pay £30 damages to the hotel's employee, as well as losing his valuables to the thieves!

April 1892 saw Harrogate suffer two jewel robberies within
a week. Firstly, one tall man and his 'thick-set' accomplice
robbed Mr Greenhalgh's premises in Market Place. With
a length of rope tightly wrapped around his fist, one of
the men smashed the glass on the window and stole a
number of items. A less successful method was used in the
follow up raid a few days later. Professional thief James
Wilson, known as 'Commercial Jimmy', broke into Miss
Anderson's jewellers in the Harrogate Arcade. Wrapping a
silk handkerchief around his fist, he smashed the window
of the shop and stole 63 gold watches. Unfortunately for
'Commercial Jimmy', he was traced to Blackburn the
following day. When searched by the police he had three
of the gold watches still in his possession – accompanied
by one blood-stained silk handkerchief! It appears that
a length of rope offers more protection than a silk
handkerchief.

The astonishing series of hotel robberies in Harrogate
continued unabated into the new century. After the death
of Queen Victoria in 1901, her son became King Edward
VII and life continued very much as before for the wealthy
visitors to the spa hotels. The extreme wealth of one guest
at the Royal Hotel proved to be too much temptation for
one of the hotel's aggrieved waiters, Frank Williams, who
also used the alias Lewis Hopkins.

Williams had been dismissed from the hotel on 9th
September 1901, due to his drunken behaviour. He was
required to finish the evening shift before leaving the
hotel's employ; and while working in the restaurant he

noticed Mr Wilson and his wife dining in the hotel's restaurant. Mr Wilson was a wealthy textile manufacturer from Leeds and his wife usually wore her impressive collection of jewellery to dinner. On that particular evening, however, she had chosen to leave her jewels in a dressing case in her bedroom.

Acting quickly, while the couple finished their meal, Frank Williams entered the Wilson's room and helped himself to silver rings, diamond brooches, gold and pearl pendants, gold chains and gold and diamond bracelets. The haul was estimated to be worth £410 (£50,000 today). Then, to avoid suspicion, Williams arranged for the hotel's groom, Fred Percival, to transport the proceeds of his theft (hidden in bags) to the railway station. At 7.15pm Williams met Percival at the station's parcel office and put the bags in a station locker. He then purchased a ticket for the 8.40pm train to Edinburgh and went for a drink at a public house in Cambridge Street, while he waited for the train. Unfortunately for Williams, the theft was noticed at the hotel and suspicion immediately fell on him. A description was quickly issued; which was recognised by a parcels clerk at the railway station. Police Constable Oliver arrested Williams as he attempted to make his getaway. At his trial he pleaded guilty, claiming he had a wife and two children to support. He was sentenced to six months hard labour.

In August 1907 a visitor at the White Hart Hotel was robbed of gold rings and a necklace worth £47, while she took tea in the hotel's lobby. It was a similar theft to one that had occurred the previous weekend, giving the police reason to believe a gang was at work in the town again. 1907 saw a string of robberies from the fashionable hotels in Harrogate and the overworked police breathed a sigh of relief when the season ended. The following year would see a huge increase in the number of heists, however, as Britain's most notorious jewel thief – 'The Quick Change Artist' - targeted the town.

James Robertson was already well known to the police, having executed several robberies at holiday resorts around the country, following his release from a long prison sentence. After a series of jewel thefts at the Swan Hydro in Harrogate in 1907, in which the thief systemically moved from room to room, a description of James Robertson was issued to the Harrogate Police and to hotel staff in the town. Robertson was described as '67 years of age, a man of grey hair and whiskers.' He was a man of many disguises, however, and the gentleman thought to be behind the string of robberies at the Swan Hydro was described as 'between 40 and 50, his hair a light auburn colour.' The man was a guest at the hotel and had registered under the name of James Berry from Preston. He was thought to be Irish, after being spotted by a maid leaving a bedroom in the hotel (which was not his own) carrying a large case. He had remarked to the maid in an Irish accent, 'how much do you think I have in here? £67. A man is lucky to have so much money'.

Mr Robertson/Berry managed to evade the police in the lobby, as his description did not match the man they were looking for. The police would not make the same mistake again. Photographs were circulated to all the major hotels in the north of England and he was eventually arrested entering the smoking room at the Great Northern Hotel in Leeds. Despite insisting, 'I am Mr James Berry from Preston', officers were not fooled. He was escorted back to Harrogate, where he was ultimately sentenced to another long prison term.

Another series of robberies from jewellers' shops followed in 1910, which were attributed to a 'man of the tramp class'. Following his arrest, it was hoped that Harrogate's hotels and jewellers could breathe a sigh of relief. Sadly, by 1911, Ogden's Jewellers in James Street had suffered a series of puzzling thefts over a period of 15 months. The missing items totalled £670 – more than £80,000 today. The matter was finally resolved when a pawnbroker, Mr Kimbell from London, became suspicious of the regular packages he had received from a Mr Ernest Clifford in Harrogate. Mr Kimbell contacted the police, who traced Ernest Clifford to JR Ogden's Jewellery shop in Harrogate. Clifford had been an employee for 15 months. When charged with the thefts Clifford said, 'Yes, unfortunately it is true. Latterly I have taken things extensively. Money difficulties led me to do it. That is all I wish to say now.' Clifford was sentenced on Thursday 7th December 1911. This case was immediately followed by yet another jewellery theft trial where a Mr Francis Anderson was convicted of having stolen 19 gold and diamond rings from a diamond merchant staying at the Temperance Hotel.

The recent first successful use of fingerprints as evidence in an English Court of Law, it was hoped, might deter thieves from their continuous targeting of premises in Harrogate. Unfortunately, fingerprinting did not assist the police following a daring theft at a house on Kent Road in 1912. the *Yorkshire Evening Post* reported the events of that night, Friday 16th August:

Mrs Bird had been entertaining one or two guests, and about 9.30pm the party left the dining-room for the drawing-room. About the same time one of the maids was on the upper floor, but just after 10 o'clock it was discovered that the bedroom door of Mrs Bird's was locked, and the electric light was full on. The alarm was raised and entrance was gained. It was then found that Mrs Bird's room had been visited by burglars, who had undoubtedly climbed on the veranda, passed through one of the guests' rooms, and reaching Mrs Bird's room, had locked the door from the inside and turned on the light. It was found that the thieves had made a good haul. Amongst jewellery missing are diamond rings of considerable value, and other rings, six valuable brooches, lockets, chains, pendants, and other jewellery. One of the pendants was dated from 1750 and is a valuable antique piece of jewellery. The burglars got away with booty valued close to £100. The robbery is thought to the work an experienced burglar, who evidently – aware of leaving fingerprints - wore gloves during the course of his operations.

The series of jewellery robberies in Harrogate even entered popular fiction, becoming part of a series of short stories featuring Detective Inspector Chance, written by George R Sims. The stories, which were tremendously popular, were serialised in *The Sketch* magazine from 1911.

The thefts continued, throughout the Great War and into the 1920s and '30s, despite Harrogate's popularity as a spa resort waning. From among the scores of other robberies over the decades perhaps the best organised and most interesting occurred at the Prospect Hotel in 1923. A wealthy London diamond merchant, Mr Pincus, was in his room at the hotel when he received a message that there was a phone call for him in the lobby. He proceeded downstairs to the hotel's reception and was kept busy on the telephone by an accomplice of the thief. Upon returning to his room nothing appeared out of place and he retired to bed. The next morning, however, on opening his cases, he discovered that diamonds and jewels to the value of £40,000 (approximately £2.5 million today) had been stolen. Suspicion immediately fell on the occupant of the next bedroom in the hotel. He had been seen leaving the hotel, and getting into a waiting car, on the previous evening. His description was immediately circulated, 'Registered under the name of L Maxwell and described as being of medium build, and about 5ft. 6in. in height, and not more than 35 years of age. He is said to be of Jewish appearance, with a sallow complexion and a broad forehead, and was dressed in a grey suit and wore a light trilby hat.'

The police immediately entered his room at the hotel, only to find his belongings and suitcases still there. Their first thought was that they had suspected the wrong man, the occupant of the room clearly intended to come back. However, the man never returned. He had evidently checked into the hotel intending to give the impression of a lengthy stay; but had departed soon after the cleverly arranged theft. The method was a carbon copy of a similar robbery in 1921 at another Harrogate hotel, when the police had opened the suitcases belonging to the occupant of the room, only to find that they were full of newspapers and cinders!

A Russian man by the name of Moischa Natensohn was arrested and admitted staying in the adjacent room to Mr Pincus, under the name of Maxwell. However, he was found not guilty at trial. The case remains unsolved and the jewellery has never been recovered.

Interestingly, the insurance company that had insured the gems for Mr Pincus initially refused to pay out on the policy. They filed a fraud claim against Mr Pincus in 1924, stating the robbery was bogus and had been staged due to some financial difficulties suffered by Mr Pincus at that time. This was not proved in court, however, and they were forced to pay out the full amount, plus damages and costs, totalling more than today's equivalent of £3 million.

That was not an end to the frightening number of jewellery robberies in Harrogate, however. Thefts have continued at the rate of two or three a year, right up until the present day, with criminals becoming ever more daring and dangerous, including the use of fast getaway cars and firearms. Mercifully, however, thanks to modern policing techniques, the authorities are now far more successful in the apprehending of offenders.

DEATH BY STARVATION

Lawrence Mansergh was born in the hamlet of Mansergh in 1836. The settlement, on the western fringes of the Yorkshire Dales National Park just north of Kirkby Lonsdale, derives its name from a combination of old English words meaning 'a plot of land for the plough or harrow', or possibly from the old French word 'mance', meaning the handle of an agricultural implement. At the time of Edward II, at the beginning of the 14th century, early records indicate a Thomas de Mansergh owning land in the area. The settlement situated there now carries the name too. By the 19th century the surname had grown to become a common one in the region.

Lawrence's father died shortly after he had been born, which left the young Lawrence without the guiding influence of a father figure. In January 1861, at the age of 25, he married 23-year-old Dorothy Bracewell, a local cabinet maker's daughter. Unfortunately, Dorothy died in the summer of 1865, possibly in childbirth, perhaps of an infection. At the time of his wife's death, however, it appears that Lawrence was already involved with another woman - given his later behaviour this would seem to be more likely than not.

It seems, too, he was already becoming desensitised to suffering and death. Within six months of his wife's death, he had moved 16 miles to the south to the market town of Settle with his new wife Mary Bowman, four years his senior. He immediately insisted that she find work in domestic service as a maid or cleaner. 33-year-old Mary was related to Lawrence's first wife Dorothy; and it is likely that he had already known her for some time.

The couple's early years of marriage were blighted with tragedy. Their first child, a daughter named Margaret, died just 12 months later. The couple then moved to Bentham, in the district of Craven, where a second child, Harry, was born but he also died within a few weeks. Lawrence and Mary then moved to Keighley where they seemed able to leave their tragedies behind them – at least for a while. Mary gave birth to two more children, Frank and Mary, who survived and blossomed. Lawrence found employment as a groom, then later as a cab driver. The work was well paid and at last, it seems, his luck had changed.

However, by 1886, Lawrence's circumstances had changed. He was now 50 years of age and rumours were rife that he was conducting an illicit affair with another woman in the town. It was later speculated in the newspapers that he had even taken out an insurance policy on his wife. Two years previously, in the summer or autumn of 1884 Mary had suffered a stroke, which had caused some paralysis and regular attacks of epilepsy. From this point onwards, perhaps because of his callous nature or perhaps because he had already begun an affair with another woman, Lawrence began to systemically neglect and imprison Mary. She was regularly locked in her bedroom, abandoned and completely dependent on her husband for food and assistance. Lawrence fed her only a starvation diet; and left her to lie in one position for so long that her muscles decayed and her limbs became crippled. He would lock the door and leave the house for long periods, presumably to visit his lover. During these periods Mary would cry out desperately to the neighbours, begging for food. On occasions they were able to assist her. However, if Lawrence returned, he would prevent them from helping her. And so, Mary's torture and agony continued, while Lawrence awaited her death from 'natural causes'. Lawrence's motives for his wife's death were strong. He was now intimately involved with a much younger woman, a Miss Horsfield, and also in well paid employment as a clerk. He frequently told his wife (it was later reported at his trial), 'to get forward with your dying,' and 'I am anxious to marry again.'

Fortunately for Mary, her appalling treatment reached the attention of the authorities and the Poor Law medical officer, magistrate and the local police officer arrived to inspect the home. The family's cottage consisted of two inner rooms and a further room at the back. The room at the rear was dark, damp, mouldy and cold, while the inner rooms were much warmer. Lawrence had chosen

one of the inner rooms for himself and kept Mary in
the most inhospitable room at the rear of the property.
After Mary's many months of agony and torture he was
finally arrested and charged with 'felonously withholding
food, nourishment, and clothing from your wife, Mary
Mansergh, and keeping her in a damp unwholesome room,
with intent to kill and murder her'.

Mary was removed to the local workhouse at Todmorden,
where it was hoped her condition would improve. A special
Petty Sessions hearing was arranged at the workhouse, as
Mary's weakened condition meant she could not attend
court to testify. Her evidence was instead given from her
bedside, in the presence of witnesses. Magistrates then
agreed that there was sufficient evidence to send Lawrence
Mansergh for trial at the Leeds Assizes in January 1887. As
the prosecution was not confident of being able to prove a
charge of attempted murder, a lesser charge was read out
to the court:

*That you, Lawrence Lambert Mansergh, did leave your wife,
Mary Mansergh, who was infirm and incapable of providing for
herself, sufficient meat and clothing, and whom it was your duty
to provide for, to wit, you failed to make proper provision for
her, whereby she became greatly disordered and injured, and her
health suffered.*

Mansergh appeared shaken but resolute, as he stood in the
dock. He pleaded 'not guilty' in a firm voice. Onlookers
commented that Lawrence's period on remand at Armley
Jail in Leeds seemed to have weighed heavily upon him, as
his appearance had become noticeably haggard.

Several legal arguments ensued between Mr Justice Day, Mr CM Atkinson for the Crown and Mr Louis Kershaw, barrister for the defence. The main points of contention being, whether any lasting harm caused to Mary Mansergh had been directly as a result of her husband's treatment, and, secondly, whether a husband was responsible for his wife's wellbeing. Ultimately, after much legal wrangling, it was decided that the indictment could proceed.

Dr Elliot gave evidence, confirming that he had visited Mary at the Mansergh's cottage in April, following a seizure, and found her in an emaciated, neglected and filthy condition. He spoke to Lawrence Mansergh and informed him that he must take better care of his wife, who was unable to do so herself. The doctor testified that Mary's paralysis had worsened and she was clearly underfed and weak. By the time that Mary's sister Alice visited her in September her condition was described as 'deplorable'. By December witnesses confirmed that Mary 'was wholly inadequately supplied with food by her husband, and that he gave no money to his wife or child'. Evidence showed that Mary Mansergh's room was 'extremely damp and unwholesome' and that she 'had sold her quilt for a shilling to purchase some bread'. When the Poor Law medical officer visited the cottage in the third week of December he found Mary on her bed, under an old horse blanket. He lifted it 'to discover the naked body of Mary covered with vermin, all skin and bone, the skin dry and parched, and the muscular tissues almost entirely worn away. The bedding was saturated with urine and faeces, and the stench was overwhelming'. Thereupon, Mary was removed to the Todmorden workhouse.

In his defence Lawrence Mansergh claimed that he had been out of work for some time, having been dismissed from his employment. However, it was demonstrated by the prosecution that on the 28th November he had visited the lodgings of, 'a Miss Horsfield and paid her the sum of 10 shillings (approximately £65 today) on account of a bastard child she had had by him'.

Following further distressing evidence regarding Mary Mansergh's condition her husband was found guilty and given the maximum sentence of two years in prison with hard labour. Mr Justice Day, in passing sentence, regretted the law did not adequately serve the seriousness of the offence, stating that 'legislation had not contemplated the possibility of a man being so devoid of common decency'.

Lawrence Mansergh was sent to the tough Armley Jail in Leeds, where he was placed in a cell with a 'dangerous lunatic' named William Sissons (who would be shortly bound for Broadmoor). Mansergh was given the role of 'watcher' (along with another cellmate James Taylor), and the pair were instructed to watch over Sissons to prevent him harming himself or others. On the night of Friday 9th March 1888, Lawrence Mansergh and James Taylor spent another night cautiously watching their unbalanced cellmate. the *Leeds Times* of the following Saturday described what happened next:

Taylor went to sleep, but the other watcher (Mansergh) remained awake. Just before ten o'clock Mansergh heard a short cough. Turning round he saw Sissons, who previously had appeared to be asleep, and who was a powerfully-built man, standing over

Taylor with a three-legged stool in both hands, raised above his head. Mansergh instantly sprang out of bed to seize Sissons, but before he had time to do this, Sissons had brought down the stool with terrific force on the right side of Taylor's head. Taylor's skull was fractured and death occurred almost instantaneously. Mansergh at once wrestled with Sissons, and, having taken the stool from him, managed to get to the bell-pull and raise an alarm. The murderer struggled desperately, the light being knocked out in the course of the tussle, but Mansergh, a stalwart young man, succeeded in overpowering him, and in holding him down until the arrival of several warders, by whom he was secured and removed to another part of the building. The surgeon of the gaol (Mr. Edwards) was called in to attend upon the unfortunate man Taylor, but a momentary examination revealed the fact that life was extinct. Blood was flowing copiously from the fractured skull, and it was evident that the blow which brought about the fatal consequences must have been delivered with terrific violence.

Lawrence Mansergh had restored his reputation somewhat. He was released from Armley Jail in January 1889. Would he emerge a changed man? He now had a chance to make amends for his previous wrongdoings. Sadly, he did anything but that.

His wife, Mary, had remained in the workhouse since her husband's incarceration. She had been classified as a pauper, with no income or outside support. Her health had still not returned due to her appalling treatment at her husband's hands. However, two weeks after Lawrence's release from prison, he visited the workhouse to see his wife. He was presented with two options by the workhouse authorities - either take his wife home and care for her himself; or have her moved to the workhouse hospital to be cared for there. He opted for the latter. Mary was sent to the workhouse hospital on 9th February, until 'it was such time that it was his pleasure to take her away again.'

Regrettably for Lawrence Mansergh, he was expected to pay a charge of eight shillings a week for her care. Six months passed and by July he had not paid a single penny, nor had he visited her once. The outstanding amount was now £8 and 8 shillings and her care had been wholly financed by the charitable union that supported the workhouse. A summons was issued for Lawrence Mansergh and an agent for the Todmorden Workhouse Poor Law Union traced him to lodgings in College Street, Keighley. A hearing was then arranged to address the matter. Lawrence Mansergh was represented by a barrister at the formal hearing, Mr JB Crossley QC. Predictably, Lawrence Mansergh claimed that he could not afford to pay the workhouse hospital bill, as he had 'suffered a good deal of sickness recently'. However, the chairman of the hearing was clearly unimpressed, 'Mr Mansergh, if you can pay an advocate such as the eminent Mr Crossley and thus can afford a luxury, you can afford to pay the guardians of the Todmorden workhouse.'

Proof was sought to determine if Mansergh had, indeed, been working since his release from prison. Keighley Police, who seemed to have some knowledge of his affairs, were able to confirm that he had been employed as a cab driver and was earning £1 per week. This was considered to be a comfortable salary for such a position in 1889.

Although £1 per week equates to approximately £120 per week today, costs of living were considerably lower in 1889, and with only limited outgoings, Mansergh could easily afford to cover his wife's workhouse hospital bills. He was left with little option but to reluctantly agree to finance his wife's care. He paid a fine, plus the outstanding arrears immediately (today's equivalent of nearly £1,000 – not an insignificant amount for a man to find at the drop of a hat) and agreed to pay for his wife's future care.

Sadly, he did not have to support his long-suffering wife for much longer, Mary passed away six months later in January 1890, aged just 52.

Lawrence did not grieve for too long it seems. By 1892 he was courting Elizabeth Alice Midgely, ten years his junior. Elizabeth, as well as being younger than her new suitor was also comfortably well off. She had the financial advantage of being supported by a guardian and had no children. Lawrence, either wishing to impress Elizabeth, or through vanity, claimed to be 51 years of age, five years younger than his actual age at the time. His deception appears to have worked, as the couple married in Keighley the following year.

Their relationship appears to have been a happy one. A decade later the couple were still together, living in Keighley, and Lawrence had found a well-paid position as a manager for the Keighley Tramway Company. Remarkably, he had grown even younger! At the 1901 census he now declared himself to be 54 years of age – the same age as his wife Elizabeth. He was actually 61 at that time.

His relationship with his two children (Frank and Mary) from his marriage to Mary is not known. It can only be imagined that it was a difficult one, knowing that they must have witnessed at first-hand his treatment of their mother. Lawrence outlived his son, however. Frank died in 1900, just two months after marrying, and still only in his 30s. His daughter, Mary, never lived with her father following his abuse of her mother. She chose instead to live with her aunt, Lawrence's sister, Margaret Seward.

Lawrence died in 1905 at the age of 65 (one wonders if his third wife ever discovered his real age?). Elizabeth married again in 1910, and lived until the ripe of age of 84, finally passing away in 1930, apparently suffering no ill effects from her twelve years of marriage to Lawrence Mansergh.

THE OTLEY MURDER (PART ONE)

1887 was an eventful year for Britain and its Empire. The country was celebrating Queen Victoria's Golden Jubilee, while across the Irish Sea the police clashed with Irish Nationalists on what would soon be called 'Bloody Sunday'. At home, the struggle of working life continued for the poorer classes, while the middle classes thrilled at *A Study In Scarlet*, the first Sherlock Holmes story. In just a few months' time, the country would be transfixed in fear as the 'Whitechapel Murders' in London filled every newspaper. However, before the country's newspaper reading public had ever heard the name 'Jack The Ripper', a tragedy took place at the end terraced cottage of William Taylor in Cambridge Street, Otley, that would traumatise the town and outrage the nation. But for the brave intervention of the Otley police, on the night of 23rd November 1887 and into the early hours of 24th November, the events may have been far worse.

William Taylor had been born in 1849 in Norwood-cum-Clifton to comfortably well-off parents. His father had been a local farmer and property owner in Otley. However, at the age of six or seven William had suffered from a serious attack of scarlet fever. Although it can now be treated with antibiotics, scarlet fever (or scarlatina as it was then known) was the leading killer of children in Victorian Britain. Although William made a full physical recovery from the infection, it left him prone to epileptic fits, headaches and mood swings. These epileptic fits occurred continuously, gradually eroding his intellectual capacity and, seemingly, his ability to work. At the age of 20 he was attacked and very severely beaten, in a fight at the village of Timble, north of Otley. Taylor suffered serious head injuries, which could have resulted in his death.

Although he again recovered, the incident further deteriorated his fragile mental state, particularly when he consumed alcohol. Despite declaring himself to be a joiner or a labourer, there is little evidence that he had worked during the 12 months leading up to the night of 23rd November 1887. Previously employed at Peter Patrick's joinery workshop in Otley, he now seemed to be 'working' only as a poacher; and his wife Hannah was forced to take on work as a 'charlady' in order to make ends meet and to provide for their three children. It was an unhappy marriage for Hannah. William was often drunk, suffered from violent mood swings and had previously been in trouble with the police on at least three occasions. In 1877 he had been convicted twice for being 'drunk and riotous', and in 1879 he was fined ten shillings for 'game trespass' (poaching).

However, his previously difficult behaviour and misdemeanours would pale in comparison to the events of

Wednesday 23rd November 1887.

The day had been uneventful in the Taylor's household. William Taylor had visited his parents' house but had returned before nightfall. It was late November and the evenings were now dark and cold. William Taylor had spent most of evening sat in front of the fire, occasionally rocking the baby in the cradle, but otherwise staring into the flames with a thunderous look in his eyes, although he did appear to be sober. Present in the house were Hannah, his wife, and two of their children, Elizabeth, aged four, and Annie, just ten weeks old. The Taylor's eldest child, William junior, aged seven, was staying with his grandfather for the night. The family had also been forced to take in a lodger, 55-year-old Ellis Brumfitt Hartley, to help ease the financial strain on the household.

William and Hannah retired to bed at midnight, as did their lodger. The baby, Annie Taylor, slept in the same room as her parents. Annie, however, was suffering from bronchitis and had been keeping the household awake by crying. Shortly after 1 o'clock Hartley, the lodger, got up and went downstairs complaining that he was unable to sleep due to the baby's crying. To warm up the room, he began to raise the fire from the dying embers. Hannah Taylor followed him downstairs, carrying the baby. She wrapped Annie in a blanket and decided to make a poultice to ease the baby's bronchitis. First, Hannah opened the front and back doors to try to create a draught to help draw the fire.

William Taylor then followed them downstairs and immediately noticed the back door from the kitchen to the yard was open. 'Why have you opened the door?', he demanded. Hannah answered, explaining that it was just to draw the fire. Taylor reacted angrily to this, and violently slammed the door closed. 'Oh, Bill! What are you going to do?', his wife exclaimed. Taylor then seized his double barrelled, breach loading shotgun, from the corner of the room, and yelled out, 'I will make it burn by having a dry shot up the chimney!' His mood and demeanour were well known to Hannah, and she immediately feared for her own, and the child's safety. She snatched up the baby, opened the back door again and rushed out into darkness of the back yard, perhaps hoping that the coal shed might provide a haven. William Taylor followed her as far as the doorway and, silhouetted by the light from the house, carefully took aim at his terrified wife. Realising that he intended to shoot her, she tried to swing around to protect the baby she was cradling in her arms. As she did so, she felt a momentary sensation on her arm as the shot grazed her. Realising that the shot had narrowly missed her she fled to the neighbouring house, still carrying the baby; and hammered frantically on the door. The neighbour, Mrs Freeman, who had already been woken by the commotion, quickly opened the door and admitted her.

As Taylor was firing at his wife, the lodger, Hartley had turned and headed for the front door, hoping to escape onto the street. As he did so Taylor spun around and fired at him. Hartley was fortunate, the shot narrowly missed him, and he ran as fast as could, also hiding in a neighbour's house. Two police officers, who were on duty at the time, PC Shippam and PC Wildman were alerted by the noise. As they reached Cambridge Street, they met the lodger, Hartley, who hastily informed them of the events. The two constables, realising the seriousness of the situation, obtained the support of Sergeants Clay and Watkins, and the men headed straight to 17 Cambridge Street where a crowd had already gathered.

Meanwhile, at the neighbour's house, with the lamps lit, Hannah Taylor and Mrs Freeman noticed blood on the blanket that she had wrapped her baby in. As she unravelled Annie's blanket they discovered more and more blood. In a panic they sent for Dr William Bennett, the local doctor, but he was unable to help and Annie died from her severe wounds approximately two hours later. There were conflicting newspaper reports at the time, some claiming that Annie had been shot in the thigh and died from massive blood loss, others stating that she had been shot in the back, causing massive internal injuries. The latter version emerged as the correct one, as the facts of the case became clearer. However, the awful truth was that William Taylor had shot and killed his own daughter.

The police officers arrived at the house but found that
Taylor had locked the front door onto the street and
the back door that opened into the yard and side lane.
It was clear that Taylor was going to offer resistance. To
complicate matters, the Taylor's other daughter, Elizabeth,
was still in the house with her father, although she appears
to have slept through all of the dramatic proceedings.
Stephen Taylor, William's brother, who lived nearby,
was summoned by the police in an attempt to persuade
William to surrender, but all to no avail. A defiant William
Taylor, shouting through the keyhole, informed the
officers that he would, 'make it warm' for anyone who tried
to enter the house.

A further two officers, Constables Wildman and
MacDonald, joined their colleagues as the news of Annie's
death reached those outside 17 Cambridge Street. Taylor
continued his threat to shoot anyone who dared to attempt
to enter the house. As day began to dawn, and the first
rays of morning sunshine began to illuminate the scene,
the constables sent for their senior officer, Superintendent
Thomas Birkhill. The Superintendent immediately took
charge, placing Sergeants Watkins and Clay along the
narrow lane at the side of the house, to guard the back
door, while PC Shippam and PC Wildman guarded the
front door. Meanwhile, inside the house, Taylor had taken
up a position occupying the bottom three steps leading to
the bedrooms, giving himself a line of sight for both the
front and back doors. The officers, at this stage, had no

idea where the Taylor's other daughter Elizabeth was, or if any harm had befallen her.

The police decided to attempt a simultaneous entry at the front and back of the house. Sergeant Watkins attempted to force the rear window, but Superintendent Birkhill pulled him back, saying, 'Take care, he may shoot again'. The Superintendent than ran through the neighbour's house from the rear, to appear at the front. With a crowbar the police had borrowed he bravely attempted to force open the lock on the front door. Unfortunately, from his vantage point inside the house and not visible to the officers outside, Taylor noticed Superintendent Birkhill through the window. Realising what was happening Taylor fired through the window at close range. The glass in the upper pane shattered as Superintendent Birkhill fell back having been hit in the head, just above his left ear. PC Wildman rushed forward and caught Birkhill in his arms. The superintendent was then carried by his men into one of the neighbouring houses, belonging to Henry Hanks, where he was attended to by Dr Bennett and two surgeons, Mr Ritchie and Mr Clarke. Despite their efforts, the trauma was severe and Superintendent Birkhill never regained consciousness. He died at 10.45am.

Meanwhile, several other officers arrived at the scene, including Inspector Crow. The crowd was persuaded to retire to a safe distance and an eerie silence fell over the street, broken only by the sound of the Taylor's dog barking in its kennel, which was in a corner of the back yard. The police officers took up safe positions, out of sight of the windows of number 17.

The silence was also noticed by William Taylor, who concluded that the police may have left. He gingerly opened the backdoor and cautiously looked around the yard. Despite Taylor's efforts to emerge undetected, Inspector Crow heard the creak of the door hinges and spotted him. Taylor, thinking that the coast was clear, came out of the back door armed with a coal shovel and a carving knife, heading for the coal shed. PC Macdonald grabbed Taylor, who screamed violently 'I'll kill you too!', and struck the officer with the shovel, smashing him in the forehead. The other officers quickly rushed in and, after a severe struggle, overpowered Taylor, finally bringing an end to the siege. To the relief of everyone the Taylor's other daughter, Elizabeth, was found safe in the house and none the worse for her ordeal. Twelve shotgun cartridges were found in Taylor's pocket and, still in the house, his shotgun had been reloaded ready for use. More cartridges were found in a kitchen drawer.

William Taylor was handcuffed and was about to be marched to the police station. However, the crowd became so hostile, screaming 'lynch him, lynch him', that Inspector Crow decided to summon a cab. A mob of several hundred people followed the cab, jeering and hooting. On the way to the police station Taylor's savage mood seemed to thaw, even becoming flippant. He told the officers, 'Don't hold me so tight; I don't want to get away. I dare say you might charge me with that. I don't care a damn, I've got my revenge.' Once at the police station he was charged with the two murders and replied in an offhand manner, 'It's all my eye and Peggy Martin' (an archaic expression, once commonly used in the north of England, meaning the whole story is unbelievable, or just village gossip), 'but I may happen to have gone a bit too far this time.'

A remand hearing and inquest were hastily arranged for the following day. It was realised that the proceedings would attract a huge amount of interest and it was decided to smuggle William Taylor into the courthouse twenty minutes before the time that the public believed he would be appearing. Following his initial arraignment and committal hearings a trial date was set for 16th February at the Leeds Assizes. In 1888 Leeds Crown Court was contained within the imposing Leeds Town Hall, which had been opened by Queen Victoria in 1858, and – as the tallest building in the metropolis – had been designed to highlight the status of the city. It must have been an ominous sight for any prisoner arriving for their trial. The participants took their places in court and the proceeding began. Mr Justice Day presided; and William Taylor was defended by Mr Waddy, QC, and his solicitor Mr Kershaw.

Much was made in court of William Taylor's fitness to face trial. When Taylor was asked to plead guilty or not guilty, he replied, 'I don't know right, sir.'

The prosecution recapitulated the events of the 23rd and 24th November 1887, whilst the defence would concentrate on Taylor's mental state and previous history of unusual behaviour.

The painful and tragic deaths of Annie Taylor and Superintendent Birkhill were re-examined, for the benefit of the jury. Some of the jury members were visibly moved. However, Taylor remained sullen and almost vacant in his expression. The defence did not contest the chain of events, instead waited passively for their opportunity to present their case.

Finally, the prosecution rested and Mr Waddy, QC, stood up in front of the hushed courtroom in his attempt (as one newspaper of the day described) to 'defend the indefensible'.

THE OTLEY MURDER (PART TWO)

And so, the 'defence of the indefensible' began in earnest, in the case of The Crown v William Taylor, 1887. In opening the case for the defence, Mr Waddy, QC, made no attempt to deny Taylor's crimes. Instead, he concentrated from the outset, on his client's fragile and unpredictable mental state.

Inspector Crow, called to the witness stand, gave evidence of an interview between Dr Ritchie from Otley (who had known Taylor for 30 years), and the prisoner which had taken place whilst Taylor had been on remand. During the interview Taylor had accused his wife of attempting to poison their child, and of 'having put something in his tea'. He also alleged that his wife had tried to poison the water supply at 17 Cambridge Street.

Dr Clarke, the physician at Wakefield Prison, and Dr William Bran Lewis, medical officer at West Riding Asylum, both stated that, based on their assessments, they would not have the slightest hesitation in signing a certificate for the prisoner's admission to a lunatic asylum.

Dr Ritchie stated that the prisoner 'was suffering from epileptic mania, which is a recognised disease. The fits brought on unconsciousness, which was succeeded by fits of anger, with homicidal or suicidal tendencies. The mania was caused by some affection of the brain, and was affected by the process of time, the mental condition becoming gradually worse and worse.'

Dr Clifford Allbutt from Leeds was called as an expert medical witness, to discuss Taylor's mental state at the time of the offence. He stated that he had seen and examined the prisoner on two occasions at the request of the defence's solicitor, once that morning and once on the previous Saturday. Dr Allbutt had endeavoured to ascertain whether the prisoner was, or was not, subject to delusions and passed his observations on to the court:

The prisoner's manner and aspect were suggestive of an epileptic and his disposition was confused. He was frequently smiling and among the answers he made to questions put was this – that he was born with four endowments, health, strength, prosperity and knowledge. He also said there were two gods, and one of these gods had forced the qualities of his personality upon him in some manner which he could not adequately explain. He was weak minded, confused, and incoherent, and when asked concerning the crime with which he was charged, he told me that he remembered nothing about the case of the child: but with regard to the murder of Superintendent Birkhill, he stated he had no remembrance of that event until some time afterwards. He had often been informed that such an occurrence had taken place, but he disbelieved it. He told me that he had heard of the circumstances from someone who came into the gaol, and who had told him what they had seen in the newspaper. He then began to think it was true and that he had done the deed, and some indistinct remembrance of the affair entered his mind. So far as I was able to tell, there was no sign whatsoever of hypocrisy on the prisoner's part in making these statements. The man's mental condition on that day (Thursday 24th November) was different, in that he was more excited.

Dr Allbutt was cross-examined by the prosecution, who asked if it was possible that Taylor was faking his insanity. Dr Allbutt replied, stating that, 'it is certainly not impossible that the prisoner was assuming the character of an insane man, when I interviewed him, but in my opinion, I do not believe I was deceived in what I observed.'

The defence asked Dr Allbutt whether he believed that, at the present time, Taylor realised the seriousness of the charge of murder filed against him? Dr Allbutt replied that he thought that he did, however he did not feel that Taylor was in a fit state of mind to give adequate instructions to his defence, or to adequately appreciate his position.

Several witnesses were produced, who all testified to Taylor's previous periods of depression, regular fits, visions, and erratic behaviour. Despite narrowly escaping being killed by Taylor, the lodger, Hartley, was called as a defence witness. He explained to the court that he had known Taylor for almost 20 years, during which time he had seen him suffer from violent epileptic fits after he had been drinking. Prior to these fits he had noticed that Taylor would become morose, low spirited and generally refuse to eat. Hartley also recalled that on previous occasions he had seen Taylor frantically searching the floor, or turning up the carpets, looking for things which he imagined to be there. Taylor had also been heard whistling, singing, and praying at night, sometimes for hours at a time.

When cross examined by the prosecution, who enquired if Taylor's unusual behaviour only occurred when drinking, Hartley explained that Taylor was usually most affected two or three days after a bout of drinking. On the Friday and Saturday prior to the murders Taylor had been drinking; but did not seem to have consumed any alcohol after that. On Sunday and Monday he appeared to be quiet and brooding, spending his time sitting by the fire. On Monday 21st November (two days before the killings), around 10pm, Hannah Taylor had called Hartley, asking him to help her with her husband, who appeared to be attempting to put his jacket on as trousers over his legs. Hartley also testified that at noon on the day before the murders, Taylor appeared to 'be trembling and his eyes were rolling about'.

Further evidence of Taylor's erratic behaviour came from PC Shippam, who had been one of the first officers on the scene. PC Shippam explained to the court that he had knocked on the door of 17 Cambridge Street, hoping to persuade Taylor to give himself up. Taylor then shouted from behind the door, 'I isn't up yet!' Shippam demanded to be let in, to which Taylor responded, 'Is it thee, lass?' When he realised it was a police officer, Taylor threatened the officer, saying, 'Come on, I's ready for thee!'

At this point in the trial PC Shippam's evidence was interrupted by an outburst from William Taylor in the dock, who shouted out to the court, 'You've been a long time making it up! I've not been asleep for a week yet. I want to see that little lass of mine.'

The minister of Otley Parish Church, Rev Thomas Greener Brooks, informed the church that he had visited the prisoner several times, by order of the Home Secretary, in order to provide some religious guidance. However, throughout all of the minister's visits Taylor had been subject to wild delusions. Rev Brooks said 'I have talked to him about his serious position, and he has told me that it was no good for me as a parson to talk to him like that: and that God Almighty had given him the knowledge and the power to commit those acts, and if he wanted to talk to anyone I had better go and talk to God Almighty. He then always used objectionable words and told me to "shut up", after saying something naughty.'

Rev Brooks added that the prisoner's parents were members of his church, and the prisoner himself had formerly attended his Sunday School.

In summing up, Mr Justice Day pointed out to the jury, 'that there could be no doubt whatever that the prisoner had killed Birkhill. The only question for them to consider was whether the evidence called upon them to add to such finding that at the time the prisoner committed the act he was of insane mind.' For the sake of clarity he outlined the legal definition of sanity (as it was in 1888) that they must adhere to in their decision making process, 'there is only one form of insanity known to law – in the sense that there is only one state of mind which was allowed by the law to relieve a person from the legal responsibilities

of crime, namely, that if a person was in such a state of mind by reason of disease as not to know the nature and quality of the act that caused death or constituted crime, then the law relieved him from that responsibility, and not otherwise. Prima facie, every person is taken to be sane, and it is therefore the prisoner's insanity that has to be established in order to relieve him from the responsibility.'

With this guidance, the jury retired. They returned 25 minutes later, declaring the prisoner guilty, but of unsound mind at the time of the killings. Following the verdict, the judge directed that the prisoner be detained indefinitely 'during Her Majesty's pleasure'. The verdict caused some disquiet outside the courthouse, with many believing that Taylor had escaped justice and should have been hanged for his crimes.

William Taylor was removed from the court by two officers, to be taken away and transported to Broadmoor Criminal Lunatic Asylum at Crowthorne in Berkshire.

There are several footnotes to the tragic events of November 1887, which add a personal and poignant touch to the story. Firstly, Superintendent Birkhill and Annie

Taylor were both buried at Otley cemetery on Saturday 26th November 1887. Superintendent Birkhill had been a hugely respected officer. Aged 57 at the time of his death, he had served in the police force for 30 years, joining as a constable in 1857 and had eventually been promoted to the rank of Superintendent. A large number of people gathered for his funeral. The inhabitants of Otley lined the route to the cemetery, shops closed, and the window blinds of houses on the route were lowered as a mark of respect. Civic dignitaries and a large contingent of police officers from across the West Riding attended.

In contrast, following the burial of Superintendent Birkhill, Annie Taylor was quietly buried in a tiny grave, with just a handful of mourners in attendance.

And what became of Hannah Taylor?

Research for this book uncovered a statement which she gave to the *Leeds Mercury* newspaper, who called at the house (rather tactlessly) on the day after her daughter's murder. They remarked that although 35 years of age, she appeared thin and older. Hannah was folding clothes at the time, and told the reporter that she was grateful that her life, and that of her other child, had been spared. The newspaper noted that she seemed conscious 'of being rid of great anxiety and dread, by the removal of her husband.' Asked to tell the story in her own words, and overcome with emotion, she replied:

We have been married ten years, but I can shed no tears over him, for he has been a scamp, and treated me brutally. On Wednesday he sat in the house most of the day rocking the cradle whilst I did the washing. All was peaceable and quiet during the evening. The baby was suffering from bronchitis, and we did not go to bed until after midnight.

After we had retired, the baby was very cross and the lodger was unable to sleep too, on account of its crying. He got up and went downstairs, and I did also, intending to put a poultice on the child's chest. My husband also got up and came downstairs. He sat down in an armchair, not saying anything in particular. The fire was not quite out, and Ellis tried to revive it. I opened both the back and front doors. The reason I did so was this: I was afraid of my husband; I never knew when he would become violent, and I thought if he became rough, we should be able to escape the more easily if the doors were open. He asked me why I had opened the doors. He jumped up and fastened the back door, saying, "Don't you meddle with that door!" I said, "Let it remain open; the fire will draw better if it is open". He thereupon got his gun, saying that he would have a shot up the chimney.

I knew what he was going to do, and I moved towards the door, having the baby in my arms. He got a cartridge out of his coat pocket, and, afraid that he would fire before I could get away, I seized hold of the gun. Being much stronger than I am, he pulled the gun out of my hand and went after Ellis, who had run out by the front door. I then got out by the back door and shut it, but he returned, pulled the door open, and fired at me in the yard. The shot struck the baby in the back, and I rushed the child into a neighbour's house. I saw nothing more of him. As I have just stated, I have always been afraid of my husband. Why? Because he has said many a time what he would do - that he would be the end of me, and that he would shoot me. He has said so, not when he has been drunk only, but also when he has been sober.

I left him for ten months, before we came to live here. We previously lived at Norwood, where we had a small farm. When I had been away from him that length of time, he found out where I was, and came and begged me to go back and live with him, saying that he would be different and work for me. But it is more than a year since he did any work, excepting for a week or two at Mr Patrick's. He has always been fond of a dog and a gun, and of beer. He did no work when we had the farm, which consisted of about 24 acres; I had all to do there. He has not been right for many a year – he drank so and carried on, and he used to have fits and foam at the mouth. I knew that he went after game, but he never bought any home; he used to sell it and drink the money.

Despite the public shame and humiliation Hannah Taylor felt, the social mores of the time often casting as much public shame on the victim as the culprit, she remained at 17 Cambridge Street for at least the next three years following the killings. However, it would not be long before she would be reminded again of the horrific events of November 1887.

Hannah Taylor had, not unsurprisingly, refused to travel to Broadmoor Lunatic Asylum to visit her husband. However, almost two years later, in September 1889, in an unexpected turn of events, she was surprised to receive an envelope in the morning post, carrying the Asylum postmark and addressed to her. With a shaking hand she opened the envelope to reveal two letters inside. One appeared to be from her husband, although she did not recognise the handwriting. The other was from Mr Nicholson, the Asylum Medical Superintendent. She first read the short note from her husband, which had been dictated and transcribed on his behalf,

Hannah

I should be very pleased for you to come and see me. It would not take you long to come. Old Satan told me to pull my eyes out, and I cannot see anything now. I have nothing else fresh to tell you.

From your affectionate husband – W Taylor

Madam,

In forwarding you the enclosed letter, written at your husband's request, I write to say that the statement he makes about having injured his eyes is, unfortunately, too true. In an attack of maniacal insanity and under the influence of delusion he destroyed the sight of his eyes with his fingers, when in his room one evening. He has, up to the present, so far recovered from the immediate effects of the injury, but something will have to be done to make his condition less uncomfortable. His sight, alas, is gone. His mind, I am glad to say, is now comparatively tranquil.

Yours – Mr David Nicholson, MD, Medical Superintendent, Broadmoor Criminal Lunatic Asylum

It appears that, whilst alone in his cell during the evening, he had gouged out his own eyeballs from their sockets, using his bare fingers, believing he had received a message from Satan instructing him to do so. His actions vindicated the decision of the courts two years previously. Taylor was clearly insane and a danger to himself and others. He would never leave Broadmoor Asylum. Neither would he ever see the remaining members of his family again. He died in 1925 at the age of 76. The complete records of William Taylor's behaviour and treatment at Broadmoor are sealed under the '100-year rule' and will not be made public until 2025.

Following receipt of the clearly shocking letter, which provided an ugly reminder of the case, Hannah Taylor resolutely remained at 17 Cambridge Street until at least the public census of 1891, when she is still recorded as living there with her children. However, by the census of 1901, then aged 59, she had moved to Bradford Road in Otley to become housekeeper for her brother, Robert.

The ramifications of the events of 23rd and 24th November were still remembered in Otley almost half a century later. In 1933 the Yorkshire newspapers published an obituary for Police Constable MacDonald (the officer who had suffered a severe blow to the head from Taylor's coal shovel). He had recently passed away, at the age of 81, following a long and distinguished service in the Otley Police. The obituary focused, almost entirely, on his role in those heartbreaking events half a century earlier and resulted in several letters to the newspaper from Otley residents, who still shivered at the memory of that night, which forever after had earned the epithet 'The Otley Murder'.

READER, I DIDN'T MARRY HIM

It may seem that the scams and frauds associated with lonely hearts, sham marriages and fake profiles, leading to those in search in love being fleeced of their hard-earned savings, is a relatively modern phenomenon. No doubt, the advent of the internet has seen a veritable explosion in this type of shameful deception. It might be imagined that a century or two ago, during the Regency and Victorian eras - the time of great romantic fiction and poetry, of moral ideals, strict courtship rituals, and family values –that this type of despicable crime would not have occurred. At least not in the relative and genteel tranquillity of the towns and villages in the Yorkshire Dales, where any romantically inclined lady or gentleman might have been more cushioned from the type of sophisticated fraudster that blights the modern world.

Sadly, you may have to think again. It appears that, almost from the moment that newspapers were first printed in Yorkshire, a series of deceptions unfolded that preyed upon those whose imagination was rapid enough to jump from admiration to love, and from love to matrimony, in a moment. Unfortunately, it seems that a single person in possession of a good fortune was ripe to be cruelly deceived. Matrimonial advertisements first began to appear in the London papers around 1810, and soon migrated to all the provincial papers in the country. Some were quite specific:

The intimations of any Lady, of unblemishable character, of an age not less than thirty, nor more than thirty-seven, and of an income equal to my own will be received with due respect.

Some, a little less fussy:

A Lady of the greatest respectability is solicitous to meet with an agreeable respectable partner for life. I do not wish for fortune, as I have an easy independency of my own.

This rapidly burgeoning business earned the Yorkshire newspapers a small fortune in advertising revenue. In fact, the industry became so profitable that it even spawned several specialist periodicals, such as *The Matrimonial Intelligencer* and *The Matrimonial News.*

The industry suffered a setback in confidence in 1827 when one William Corder married a lady called Mary Moore. The couple had met after Mary had answered Corder's reassuring advertisement:

To any female of respectability, who would study for domestic comfort, and willing to confide her future happiness in every way qualified to render the marriage state desirable.

The couple married one week later; only for Mary to discover that Corder had brutally murdered his first wife and buried her body in a barn.

To offer some redress, the book *Some Remarks on Matrimonial Advertisements Being an Inquiry into their Use and Abuse*, published in 1832, offered young ladies some timely advice on how to proceed when personally answering a matrimonial advertisement:

It is presumed that the gentleman – if interested – will have proposed. A reasonable time is then allowed for the lady to make up her mind, and take the sense of her friends and advisers, and usually within a month a definitive answer is received. If unfavourable, she simply declines the overtures, no particular reasons being assigned, that the feelings of neither party may be wounded; of course the correspondence is mutually delivered up, the negotiation ends, and ever after remains an inviolable secret.

But despite continuing incidences of misrepresentation and downright villainy, matrimonial advertisements continued to gain in popularity as the century progressed. In fact, young ladies in search of love sought some insight elsewhere. During 1883, two young women from Otley (described by the *Leeds Times* as 'not ugly ones, but appear to be desperately hard up for sweethearts'), sought some divine inspiration in their search for men of marriage material. Mary Haverly and Maria Piper journeyed from Otley to the Leeds Fair in order to visit fortune teller Catherine Murray.

The two girls visited the fortune teller who told them that she required a new dress from each of them in order to tell their fortune properly. They promptly went away, both purchased a new dress and returned. Catherine Murray thanked them, and promised them 'a nice young man each' if they placed £1 each (approximately £130 today) in a handkerchief she had already laid out on the table. Mary and Maria promptly did this; Catherine Murray knotted the handkerchief together and handed it back to the girls. The fortune teller then warned them that, 'your sweethearts await you if you did not untie the handkerchief until the day you had met your future husbands'. After some time passed, and the ladies were still unattached, they unknotted the handkerchief to find it empty. Angry at their own gullibility, Mary and Maria pursued Catherine Murray through the courts resulting in the fortune teller being sent to prison for one month.

In late 1899 an advertisement began to appear in the *Yorkshire Post* which attracted the attention of a comfortably well-off young gentleman from the village of Grassington. The advertisement read as follows:

INTELLIGENT, ATTRACTIVE, YOUNG LADY wishes to meet honourable gentleman; with the object of matrimony. Please respond via the offices of the newspaper to "Poste Restante, Douglas, Isle of Man", where I am presently residing and to which I visit two or three times a year.

The young man, wishing to find love and perhaps a little lonely replied immediately, enclosed a photograph of himself and expressing his interest in meeting the mysterious young lady. We can presume that the distance involved was not a concern when compared to his higher motives. He waited anxiously until he received a reply, which arrived written in a delicate feminine hand and contained in a scented envelope. As he unfolded the letter, he found a portrait photograph of a beautiful young lady concealed inside,

Sherwood Terrace, Douglas, Isle of Man, December 15, 1899

Dear Sir,

A thousand thanks for your answer to my advertisement, also for the photograph, which, I am sorry to note, you do not consider is like yourself. I am glad to receive it nevertheless, as it brings into my life a new existence. I hope and trust our acquaintance will continue to grow until the mutual objects of each shall have been attained. It seems to me as if there were already some bond of sympathetic affection really binding us together. I know from your letter you must be a man whom any woman would delight to love, honour, and obey. I should be glad to come to Yorkshire to meet you. We could then see whether the affinity between our souls is striking enough to unite us for all time. I enclose my photograph. It shows me as I truly am- Does it suit you?

I am, I may say, one of the unconventional kind. I am yet young and inexperienced. We must see each other to know if there is any use in our continuing this correspondence along the lines of custom before reaching the goal of our ambitions. I am, unfortunately, financially poor. If you will send me £3 (approximately £400 today) to pay my expenses I will come, and over a delightful tete-a-tete we can see what is best. Do not send a post office order, I am known here at the post office, and would not have my guardian know what I am about to do. And believe me, always sincerely yours, - Maud Gerridge

The young gentleman sent his reply to the Douglas Post Office, requesting a meeting with the mysterious Maud Gerridge.

My Dearest Maud

I feel that we know each other's souls so well that I can offer you more affection than in a single day than most men can do in a lifetime – to borrow the words of another Yorkshireman with power in his soul.

I have enclosed £3 and I hope we can make such arrangements that will speed the moment that we can be together. I have now your photograph, which will not allow me to know you instantly, but has, I must confess, hastened my desire to meet with you.

Yours in ardent admiration – MA

Sadly, and predictably the young gentleman received no further communication from the 'young lady' and finally, in a state of despair, visited the offices of the *Yorkshire Post*. He was surprised and distressed to discover, not only a handful of other angry gentleman enquiring at the desk about the same advertisement, but that the newspaper had received over 200 other complaints from aggrieved male suitors from Shipley, Ilkley, Harrogate, Richmond, Otley, Sheffield, Bradford and Leeds. The matter was reported to the Yorkshire Police, unfortunately the address in Douglas and the name Maud Gerridge proved to be entirely false. After the trail ran cold, Scotland Yard continued the investigation, however the young lady was never traced, if indeed, the fraud was actually perpetrated by a lady. No further advertisements appeared in the Yorkshire press from Maud Gerridge, although it highly likely that the advertisements continued to appear elsewhere in the country, perhaps using another name.

It seems it was not just the lonely male population of Yorkshire that suffered at the hand of an unscrupulous manipulator of their affections. Many young ladies of Victorian Yorkshire society were duped by unfeeling conmen, such as the serial bigamist William Gordon Pearson. The 47-year-old engineer from Brompton, during a ten-year period from the mid-1880s onwards, managed to find enough time to become engaged to at least 16 girls (to whom he had faithfully promised marriage), and to marry at least a further four. All of the ladies were seduced by Pearson, in the Hydro hotels of Harrogate, Ilkley, Ripon and York.

Pearson would find what he determined to be a single lady, preferably wealthy, and lavish his attentions on her, eventually proposing marriage. After his proposal was accepted Pearson would persuade the young lady, or her family, to purchase presents, furniture, clothes and expensive meals as gifts for the happy couple. Following their supposed wedding, the couple would book into expensive rooms, at hotels such as the Old Swan Hotel in Harrogate or the Scarborough Hydropathic Hotel, and spend a blissful wedding night together. On awakening the next day, he would abscond on the pretext of taking an early morning stroll and never be seen again. To those who became engaged to Pearson, on a promise of marriage, he would remain with them only until their finances were

exhausted, at which point he would promptly disappear;
never to be seen again, leaving the young lady penniless
and with a ruined reputation.

In all probability, he committed many more offences of
bigamy than the 20 which were declared. It is likely that
there were many victims of his heartless frauds that never
came forward for fear of bringing shame upon their
families.

Exactly how William Pearson managed to evade capture
for so long is probably explained by the staggering number
of aliases he used – William Lancaster, William Gray,
Pearson Williams, Duncombe Green, Garnett Beaumont,
William Hartley and Hartley Williams being just a
selection. He was finally arrested in January 1896 after
leaving a Ripon hotel early in the morning (with his new
wife still asleep in bed), having run up a bill for food and
accommodation to the tune of £11 7s 9d (today's equivalent
of approximately £1,500). Pearson had also obtained a
gold watch and chain from a nearby jewellers. The police
were informed, who managed to piece together several
stories and descriptions, which all appeared to be of the
same man. He was later arrested at a Manchester hotel and
brought back to Yorkshire to face trial.

On 3rd February 1896 he was brought before Scarborough
police court, at which a huge crowd of female spectators
had gathered to witness the dashing lover who had
managed to sweep so many young ladies of their feet.
According to the *York Herald* of the following day, they
were sorely disappointed:

Those present who expected to find in him an Apollo like figure or even an insinuating Don Juan were doomed to disappointment. He is short, flabby of features, nearly 50 years of age, with a strong grey beard and an unhealthy complexion, and he trembled most violently on being ushered into Court.

Pearson was remanded for trial, after refusing to enter a plea of guilty or not guilty; and removed to York Castle Prison amid the booing and jeering from the female audience gathered outside the Police Court.

At the trial, William Pearson refused legal representation, choosing to remain silent instead. Mr TP Hart, for the prosecution, explained to the court the way in which Pearson had duped both the hotels he stayed in, and his various wives and fiancées:

William Pearson, the prisoner, obtained the credit of the establishment, on the false representations that he was the owner of Brompton Manor, near York, a shooting estate near Helmsley known as Gatherley Castle, and also a public-house at Otley. At the expiration of the fifth week of his stay at the establishment, Pearson would declare to the manager that his money was not expected to arrive for another few days. "Would credit be allowed until then?" On the strength of being a property owner he was allowed to break the usual rules of the establishment. He would then abscond without trace, having run up a considerable debt.

William Pearson drove a horse and dog-cart, which he claimed belonged to Brompton Manor, and no doubt formed part of his subterfuge. However, Mr Hart called James Hutchinson, the Deputy Chief Constable of the

North Riding of Yorkshire police, to the stand. He was able to confirm that Pearson did not own any property in Yorkshire, that there was no such place as Brompton Manor, that no one had either heard of Gatherley Castle, and that the horse and dog-cart belonged to an Ilkley livery company.

William Pearson still refused to speak or to call any witnesses for his defence, at which point he was bound over to face trial on further charges. He was offered bail at an amount of £50 for each charge. Pearson explained to the judge that, 'if I am let free, I have some property which I can dispose of between now and the trial, which will cover my bail.' After a grimace from the magistrate, Pearson was promptly removed to the cells!

As his next trial Pearson's identity came to light. Under examination he admitted that his real name was William Lancaster and that he taken Croft Hall, near Darlington, on a three-year lease in 1890. After having run up considerable debts, he claimed to have invented a new method for the production of gas; in which he then persuaded several gentleman and prospective wives to invest in. Pearson/Lancaster claimed that the invention would net him around £13,000 – enough, he thought, to attract both future investors and potential wives. After using several false names to obtain credit, he moved to Ilkley under the name William Garnet. However, whilst living at Ilkley, another of his marriage scams saw him sentenced to twelve months' imprisonment for obtaining money by false pretences.

He continued to protest his innocence, claiming that his other wives were either dead, or that they had left him, and he had assumed that they were dead.

Ultimately, he was found guilty and sentenced to a further twelve months' imprisonment.

Despite this, the matrimonial industry continued to blossom into the new century. Newspapers across the county even began to publish warnings:

All women who ever answered a matrimonial advertisement, or intend to ever do so, should remember: No man who has the ability or means to support a wife in comfort needs to advertise for one.

Ultimately it seems, we are all fools in love. For the young ladies and gentlemen of Yorkshire, and the rest of the country, the desire for marriage continued to remain the triumph of hope over experience, as these advertisements no doubt testify:

Some sweet damsel is earnestly requested to claim the unbestowed affections of one who is tall, well educated, maybe attractive and aged 25 years. Will any pretty maid have compassion?

Merry hearted girl, highly domesticated and passably good looking, but a good cook and economical housekeeper.

Jack, aged 27, dark, tall, blue eyes, heavy moustache, fond of boating, would like to meet a lady with a view to early marriage.

Mabel, a parlourmaid, aged 29, tall, dark eyes and pale face would like to correspond with a tradesman. I am not pretty, but quite domesticated, and would make a good useful wife.

Sweetheart, aged 20, medium height, blue eyes, good tempered, would like to correspond with gentleman, aged 21 to 40, either dark or fair, any height from 5 feet 8 inches to 6 feet 1 and a half inches; milksops, cork legs and beards objected to. Photo required.

A tall gentleman, aged 23, with dark hair and eyes, is anxious to meet with an eligible partner for the journey of life. The lady must be fair, amiable, and educated. Plumpness essential.

Neptune, aged 35, good looking, smart appearance, Captain of a crack steamer, desires to correspond with a true hearted, fair, plump, pretty, English girl.

Willie, artistic, clever, literary, lovable to a fault, wicked eyes, Byronesque, good birth, wishes to correspond with a fair girl of refined manners.

A Lady, aged 22, well developed form, cheerful, musical, and a daring horsewoman, desires to correspond at once with a gentleman of moderate income.

A young Lady, aged 18, good figure, not bad looking, thoroughly domesticated, and in fact, all that a man can wish for, would like to correspond with a tall, handsome, dark gentleman, with a view to matrimony. Must have good teeth.

After picking your way through the minefield of Victorian matrimonial advertisements, searching for your Fitzwilliam Darcy or your Bathsheba Everdene, only one question remains. Would you swipe left or right?

GHOSTS IN THE DALES

The tranquillity and splendour of the Yorkshire Dales are a welcome sight to many a traveller looking for a break from the monotony of city life. However, behind the raw beauty of the crags and rolling moorlands hides a darker and more sinister side. There are myths and legends, some of a more supernatural and unearthly derivation, but many based on historical events.

In the east of the Dales, just south of Leyburn, lies the small community of Coverham, by the ancient bridge that crosses the River Cover. Looking over the drystone walls that line Coverham Lane, the passer-by can see the disused 13th century Holy Trinity Church. Despite the redundant nature of the building, the peaceful and well-tended churchyard contains two graves of interest. Firstly, the resting place of the man who dug his own grave, and secondly, the grave of the 'Black Lady of Coverham', also known as the 'Black Lady of Middleham Moor'.

The story of the 'Black Lady' had persisted in that corner of the Dales for over two hundred years; and was thought to be little more than a fanciful tale. Locals spoke of a beautiful young girl from the village who fell in love with the wealthy son of the local squire. While their respective parents slept, the girl wrapped herself in a black lace shawl and, under cover of darkness, crossed Middleham Moor to meet her lover at the gates of Cotescue Park. However, the young couple's secret was uncovered. Not by their respective parents, but by another young girl who had suspected a lovers' tryst.

Unfortunately for the clandestine young couple, the other girl was madly jealous, wanting the squire's son for herself. She informed the squire's son that his secret lover was involved with another man. Overcome with sorrow, jealousy and rage, that night the squire's son hid behind a corner in the wall of Cotescue Park and waited for his lover. When she passed the corner where he had hidden himself, obscured by the dark and the shadows, he leapt out. With a blunt instrument in his hand, he smashed it down on her skull. He then hauled her still-warm body to an isolated spot on the moor, before burying it in a shallow grave. After covering his tracks, he returned home.

The legend of the 'Black Lady' persisted for at least 150 years, with many locals and visitors claiming to have seen a ghostly figure in a black lace shawl gliding across the moor in the direction of the Cotescue Park. Gradually, fewer and fewer came to believe in the story, as it was handed down through the generations, until one day in the 1930s...

A party of turf cutters were digging at an isolated spot on Middleham Moor when they unearthed a skeleton, buried in a shallow grave. The remains had clearly been in the ground for a long period of time. As well as the shock of discovering a dead body, the men noticed that the victim had been wrapped in a black lace shawl.

The remains of the victim from the shallow grave were re-buried at Holy Trinity Church in the village. From this

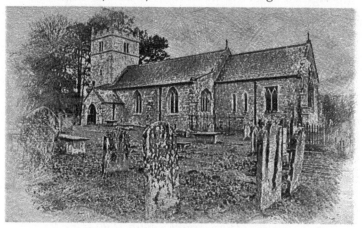

point onwards, stories of the 'Black Lady' resurfaced. There were a series of sightings in which the ghost of the murdered woman was seen to rise from her grave in the churchyard, before silently and eerily making her way across the moor in the direction of Cotescue Park, apparently still seeking her lover. According to witnesses, when the apparition of the 'Black Lady' reaches the corner in the wall where she was murdered, she promptly vanishes.

Sightings of the ghost have been reported in the newspapers and, when a local man working on a nearby farm died of a heart attack during the 1930s, it was speculated that he may have died of shock on seeing the ghost of the 'Black Lady'.

Journeying from Harrogate to Skipton along the A59, the road passes the Fewston and Swinsty Reservoirs on the left. At the south end of the Swinsty Reservoir lies Swinsty Hall. Although the reservoir was not constructed until 1874, the house is much older and dates from the 16th century. According to *The Haunted Homes and Family Traditions of Great Britain* (1897), by John Ingram, and *The History of the Timbles and Snowden* (1864-1895,) by William Grainge, the house is haunted by a man called Henry Robinson who, according to legend, bought the property with the profits he had gained from the sale of goods looted from the empty houses of the dead in London, during the bubonic plague. Grainge wrote in 1864:

In the picturesque valley of the Washburn, high up on the right bank, in the parish of Otley, stands Swinsty Hall. It is a large building, in a kind of Elizabethan architecture, and, on its first creation would, doubtless, be considered a great, grand, and glorious mansion, with its many gables and multitudinous windows. The greatest wonder is to see it here at all, in such a lonely place. It has been built in a substantial manner, and at a heavy cost.

Swinsty Hall has fallen somewhat from its high estate in modern times, stripped of its antique furniture, and now is occupied by the families of four farmers (with a rambling ghost or two), the barns and outhouses clustered around give it quite a singular and unique appearance.

The supernatural legend connected with Swinsty Hall was described by William Grainge in 1864 as follows:

The builder of the Hall was a man of the name of Henry Robinson, who, in his youth, was a poor weaver, and resided in a humble cottage near where the Hall now stands. This cottage, now doing duty as a cow-house, yet remains to vouch for the truth of the story.

According to *The Haunted Homes and Family Traditions of Great Britain*, Henry Robinson travelled to London to seek his fortune:

This young man left his humble home, at a time when the plague was raging in that city; when death had left many houses totally uninhabited and desolate, wherein no survivors were left to bury the dead, and no heirs to claim their wealth. Our north country adventurer seeing this state of things, for- getting himself amid the general mourning and confusion, took possession of the gold thus left without an owner, to such an extent, that he loaded a wagon and team of horses with the wealth thus acquired; with which he returned homeward, and, in due time, again reached the place of his birth. But the story of the plague had reached the place as soon as himself and his gold, and none of his former neighbours would admit him into their dwellings, for fear of contagion; so he took up his abode in a barn, which still remains. In order to cleanse his gold from any infectious taint which might possibly cling to it, Robinson washed the whole carefully in the Greenwell Spring, which well yet remains, bearing the same name.

Swinsty Hall had been built in the Elizabethan style for a wealthy merchant named Francis Wood around 1575.

However, Henry Robinson gradually acquired the Hall and all its estates from Francis Wood between 1590 and 1596, when Wood, it seems, was unable to repay monies he had borrowed from Robinson. Robinson, it appears, was as ruthless in business as he was in the original acquisition of his wealth.

In the early 1600s Henry Robinson drastically, and in a rather ostentatious manner, remodelled the house, after which it remained in the Robinson family until 1772, when it passed by marriage into the Bramley family. In the 1870s, it was sold to Leeds Corporation to facilitate the construction of the Swinsty and Fewston reservoirs.

Yet there still have been many alleged sightings over the past century or so. This description from the *Yorkshire Post* in 1900, explains that Henry Robinson could not:

Cleanse himself, so readily as he did his gold, from its contamination: his troubled spirit still haunts the old spot. At certain times, those who are gifted with the faculty of seeing apparitions, may behold the apparition of Robinson bending over the Greenwell Spring, and striving to cleanse his strangely acquired coin even more spectral than himself. There he bends, and rubs, and rubs, and rubs away at his ghastly spoil, and never seems satisfied that it is freed from its taint, or, perhaps, from its stains: who knows?

However, despite the legend persisting for 400 years, its origins have been called into doubt. It seems that a Ralph Wood owned the original Swinsty Hall. In 1575, during the preparations for the marriage of his son Francis Wood and Ellen Sorell, he arranged for the bride's father, Henry Sorrell, of North Grange, to fund the construction of a new house for the recently married couple. It appears that Henry Robinson did not acquire Swinsty Hall until later on, when he foreclosed on a loan to Francis Wood, in around 1590, although it is not clear for what reason the loan had been granted, since Swinsty Hall had already been built by that date. Henry Robinson was then responsible for the major remodelling of the house at the beginning of the 17th century. Previous historians have cast doubt on the fact that Robinson had originally acquired his wealth by the systematic looting of houses during an outbreak of the 'Black Death', or bubonic plague, in London. This uncertainty is usually based on the chronology traditionally associated with the story. The first recorded major outbreak of the bubonic plague in London was 1603 when 30,000 people perished. This was 13 years after Robinson was thought to have acquired Swinsty Hall. However, this is not a fatal objection to the story as bubonic plague first arrived in England in 1348 and outbreaks continued at frighteningly frequent intervals after that, fuelled by poor sanitation, overcrowding and medical ignorance. Thousands were killed in regular outbreaks from 1350 to 1670 (including the 'Great Plague' in 1665-6). There were major reccurrences throughout the period of this story, particularly in 1563, 1589, and 1593. In fact, it is unlikely that a single year passed during that 300-year period without a significant number of deaths occurring.

So perhaps, if you hear the clink of coins somewhere close to the banks of the Swinsty Reservoir, remember that the story behind the guilt-ridden ghost of Henry Robinson may have some basis in fact after all.

Swinsty Hall eventually reverted to private ownership and is now a grade I listed building.

To the west of Richmond, close to Gunnerside and the hamlet of Ivelet, the single span Ivelet Bridge is a grade II listed structure. Despite being the most picturesque and attractive of bridges, dating from 1687, the tranquillity of its appearance masks its sinister secret. The Ivelet Bridge was once an important crossing point on the 16 mile 'Corpse Way', or 'Coffin Path' from Muker to the churchyard at Grinton. Many centuries ago, the graveyard at Grinton was the only patch of consecrated ground where a grieving family could bury their loved ones. Relatives, or a bearer or carrier, would be forced to carry the body of the deceased along the length of 'Corpse Way',

usually contained in a wicker basket. Resting points were placed along the way, including the coffin stone which now sits beside the bridge. Another early Christian tradition, especially common in the north of England, required that a large black dog should be buried at the north of the churchyard, or at a crossroads along a 'Corpse Road', to act as a guardian spirit for those buried there. The Ivelet Bridge is said to be haunted by one such hound, a black headless dog, which runs up the bridge, jumps the wall and into the River Swale below, before disappearing. There have been many witness accounts of the headless dog over the previous two centuries. However, although the apparition seems to be benign in nature, a sighting is not necessary a welcome thing, as it is said to be a harbinger of death or bad luck.

Stories of supernatural black dogs are common in many parts of the world. Gradually, with the passage of time, the legends have grown. The otherworldly beasts are commonly described as huge, ferocious animals; haunting churchyards and lonely country lanes, with glowing, piercing eyes, and sharp white teeth and claws. Over many years these demonic hounds have been known by many names, particularly in the Yorkshire Dales - Barghest, Hell Hounds, Grims, Goblin Dogs, Padfoots, and Gabriel Hounds.

Surprisingly, the Yorkshire Dales contain no less than five such legendary Hell Hounds. One such legendary beast is said to haunt Troller's Gill, a limestone gorge, close to the village of Skyreholme, five miles south east of Grassington. The gorge is named after the supposed existence of trolls who used to live there. Legend has it that Troller's Gill is the home of a mythical and monstrous black dog with large teeth and claws, known as the Barghest, who can turn a man to stone with one look. The story of the Barghest is said to have inspired Sir Arthur Conan Doyle to create his most famous novel *The Hound of the Baskervilles*. Indeed, stories of such beasts have continued to engage the imagination of authors to the present day, including JK Rowling.

At nearby Grassington, a huge, rainbow eyed black barghest is said to haunt the fields surrounding the town. The hound emits a ghostly, rattling sound and is reputedly to be the size of a horse. One wonders if the Black Horse Hotel in Grassington takes its name from the legendary creature! The town of Skipton also has a similar legend of a ghostly hound, completely silent, yet enormous in size – described as being 'like a huge black horse' -which patrols the fields around the town. Is it a coincidence, then, that Skipton also boasts an inn named The Black Horse?

Legends of ghostly black dogs are not just historic, it seems. As recently as 2001 witnesses reported seeing a large, featureless black dog crossing the A684 between Leeming Bar and Northallerton, as one leaves the Dales. The shadow-like animal caused drivers to slow down and was described as 'strange and otherworldly'.

Finally, a recent and unusual ghostly encounter. At one of the highest and most exposed areas of moorland along the Pennine Way, where the Yorkshire Dales meet

the North Yorkshire Moors, sits Britain's highest public
house. The Tan Hill Inn, near Reeth, sits 1,723 feet above
sea level and is one of the county's most haunted public
houses. Although the current building dates from the 17th
century, there has been a building at the location for much
longer. Because of the Tan Hill Inn's isolated location,
many travellers, trapped by deep snow, have sheltered
there, sometimes for days. The Inn has also been used as
a temporary mortuary when bodies were carried in from
the moors, having frozen to death. Reported sightings
by witnesses maintain that several of these unfortunate
individuals are still in residence as ghosts. The Tan Hill
Inn is also thought to be haunted by a more recent, 20th
century ghost, Mrs Susan Peacock. Installed as landlady in
1903, Susan Peacock was notorious for keeping a loaded
pistol behind the bar to frighten off argumentative
customers. She was licensee for almost 40 years, until
her death in 1937. Reputedly buried behind the Inn, she
appears when alterations are undertaken at the Inn to
ensure they are being suitably conducted. In recent years,
during some building renovations, her ghost has been
blamed for a television set in one of the rooms constantly
switching itself on without explanation.

Paranormal investigators have been active at the Inn as
recently as 2019, after ghostly apparitions were spotted in a
photograph taken by a customer. A visitor took a picture of
her dog, Daisy, sat in front of the pub's fire. However, when
the dog's owner looked carefully at the photograph, she
noticed what appeared to be a skull in the fireplace.

The photo was posted on the Tan Hill Inn's social media pages and immediately caused a sensation, with both staff and customers spotting three other sinister faces hidden in the photo. Other visitors contacted the Inn with their experiences. A lady staying at the pub, just a couple of years earlier, claimed that she had woken in the middle of the night to find a woman standing at the end of her bed, dressed in what appeared to be 1930s clothing. It has been suggested that this was the ghost of former landlady Susan Peacock.

Others have smelt the distinct odour of pipe smoke, despite being alone in the room at the time, or when nobody in the building was smoking.

It seems the brooding moors and hills of the Yorkshire Dales are home to as many unexplained sightings as they were in the days before scientific enlightenment and modern technology. Perhaps they are not yet ready to reveal all their secrets to an intrigued public.

HORROR AT PATELEY BRIDGE

The pleasant market town of Pateley Bridge sits next to the River Nidd in Nidderdale, close to Harrogate.

Wednesday 18th July 1906 had been another warm and quiet day in the town. The Edwardian summer had been a hot one and the uncomfortable heatwave continued, fraying tempers. Nevertheless, life carried on very much as before for the inhabitants of the town. Meanwhile, Parliament debated tightening the Sunday Trading Laws and the new Liberal government of Henry Campbell-Bannerman celebrated their large majority at the recent election.

James Dougill, a 44-year-old labourer, lived with his wife, Catherine, and their seven children in a small, stone cottage at 86 Tanners Row, behind the High Street. Relations between the couple during their 20-year marriage had been strained almost from the beginning. James Dougill was a difficult man to live with, suffering from black moods and a dependence on alcohol. Although he had attended the well-respected Pannal Ash College at Harrogate, he had struggled to hold down meaningful employment since leaving, mainly working as a casual labourer.

Despite the couple's difficulties, it had been a quiet and peaceful evening in the household. There had been nothing in James Dougill's behaviour to suggest anything out of the ordinary. The family had all retired to bed and were asleep. Catherine Dougill went to bed around 11pm, taking her baby daughter with her. Her husband remained downstairs. One of the Dougill's other daughters, 15-year-old Susannah, also slept in another bed in her parents' room. At around 3am she was woken suddenly by the sound of her mother screaming out in pain. In the dim light, Susannah was aware of a shadowy figure hurrying past her bed, leaving the room, and rushing down the stairs. Frightened, she ran out of the room and down the stairs, just in time to see her father leaving by the front door. She looked outside the door; but could see nothing but the shadows caused by the moonlight. By this time, woken by the commotion, Susannah's siblings were crying and screaming too. She ran back into the house to see what had happened to her mother.

Meanwhile, the children's uncle, William Storey, who lived in a neighbouring cottage and worked with James, had been aroused by the frantic screams of the children and had hurriedly run out into the street, still dressed in his night attire. He quickly searched the yard and outbuilding but could see no sign of James Dougill. The children implored him to come and help their mother, so he rushed inside. Catherine Dougill was lying prostrate in the bed, bleeding heavily from an ugly wound to the abdomen. There were a series of cuts on her wrists and fingers (which appeared to be defensive wounds). On the floor next to

bed lay a blood-stained carving knife. Catherine Dougill attempted to speak and William Storey leant forward, straining his ears, in an effort to hear her. In an agonising tone she whispered, 'He has done it'.

The victim's sister, Mrs Dunn, was fetched by one of the children. She told the family that she had just seen their father James Dougill running down the street, away from the house. Catherine Dougill grabbed her sister's arm and breathlessly explained the horrific events of the night. These words that Catherine Dougill uttered to her sister would later be recounted in court by Mrs Dunn, as the deposition of a dying woman:

James went downstairs dressed. In a few minutes he returned to the bedroom, blew out the candle, and stood over me. He said "can you say you have done right by me?". I replied that I was tired of this silly talk. He pulled down the bedclothes and struck me in the stomach with something sharp. He had often threatened me, and had gone so far as to pull out a knife before. He also hit me on the arms and the wrist. We struggled, then he rushed out of the room, and I didn't see him again.

Catherine Dougill was left in a critical condition by the attack and the doctor described her chances of a recovery as 'very remote'.

Meanwhile several police constables began a search of the surrounding area. They scoured all the local outbuildings, back yards and alleyways but could not locate James Dougill. Local rumours began to circulate in Pateley Bridge. Whilst Catherine Dougall was known to be a mild mannered and likeable person, her husband was known to be unpredictable by many of the Patelely Bridge residents. It was speculated that mental illness had long affected James Dougill's side of the family. Gossip spread that Dougill's father, uncle, and cousin had all taken their own lives. Meanwhile, the search had been fruitless. A further 24 hours had passed; and the police were still unable to trace James Dougill, either dead or alive.

Finally, on Saturday, a full 48 hours after the attack on his wife, James Dougill was located. He was discovered by police officers, trapped in an old mineshaft which formed part of a now disused lead mine, close to the Knaresborough to Pateley Bridge road. All around the town, the local landscape was scarred with the remnants of many such mines. The mine had closed several years earlier, during the early 1880s, and in the time that had elapsed since shutting down it had become a refuse tip for locals. At the time of its closure in the 1880s, the mineshaft had measured 120 feet in depth. However, for the previous 15 years or so, locals had filled the shaft with all sorts of foul smelling refuse, including dead dogs and cats and even the carcass of a pony. James Dougill had either jumped or fallen into the disused shaft. Fortunately for him, the depth of the shaft now measured only 70 feet. A 50 feet cushion of rotting refuse had broken his fall. It was, however, a miracle that he was not killed.

After hearing cries for help, Inspector Fairburn, assisted by three constables, was lowered down into the mineshaft. It was to be an experience he would not easily forget. A plank was placed across the mouth of the pit, which measured about seven feet in diameter. The three constables then lowered the Inspector carefully down the hole. The strain on the men lowering the officer was huge and several times they almost lost their grip on the rope, as they struggled to keep their footing. Luckily, they managed to prevent Inspector Fairburn from plunging to his death in the blackness of the shaft. As he descended the stench almost overpowered him. Once at the bottom, James Dougill was overjoyed to see the police officer, and shook his hand. Dougill's medical condition was poor and he appeared to have lost a great deal of blood. Gingerly, and with huge difficulty, Dougill and the Inspector were slowly winched up from the shaft. Once on the surface Dougill's injuries were attended to. He was then arrested and gave the following statement to Inspector Fairburn:

I did not mean to murder her, but she told me I dare not strike her with anything. Immediately after the occurrence I ran, without my boots on, to the pit shaft. I reached the top in a few minutes, crept under a covering of bushes and brambles, so as not to leave a trace of my whereabouts, and then I dropped into the pit. As I fell, I touched the sides, which seemed to break my fall. I reached the bottom in no time and dropped with a thump.

Dougill had been rendered unconscious by the fall and remained in that state until midday on Friday, approximately 30 hours after the stabbing of his wife. 'On coming around I shouted for help', he continued in his statement, 'and the third time the call was answered.'

Dougill appeared at the Harrogate Police Court on Saturday morning. Described by the *Yorkshire Mercury* as:

A slightly built man, with haggard cheeks and half-closed eyes, he was the picture of despair and misery. His head and his left hand were heavily bandaged and his closely cut whiskers were almost white, despite the fact he is only 44 years of age. He moaned the whole of the time he was in court and was allowed to sit while evidence was given.

James Dougill was placed on remand while the incident was investigated, and it was decided whether to additionally charge him with the further offence of attempting to commit suicide (it was not until The Suicide Act of 1961 that those who tried, and failed, to take their own lives were safe from the threat of prosecution).

The following morning, Sunday 22nd July 1906, Catherine Dougill succumbed to her injuries. She was just 44 years old. The charge against James Dougill was now one of murder.

A Coroner's Inquest was held the next day at Ripon. The only witness called was William Storey, Catherine Dougill's brother, who was asked to describe the events of the early hours of 19th July and to provide some background on James Dougill:

Around half past three on Thursday morning I was awakened by a scream. After looking for James I went straight into my sister's bedroom, and found her lying on the bed. I asked her what was the matter, and she said "Oh, he has stabbed me. Run for the doctor." I heard no disturbance that night until I heard the scream. I had heard disturbances before though. Several times Dougill had come home 'fresh' and thrown furniture and clothing out of the door. I have heard him threaten to take the lives of his children, and to tear their insides out. I have never heard him threaten his wife. I was working with him up to 5.30pm on the Wednesday evening. He was sober, but excited. He said to me that some men, working at another building farther up the garden, were looking at his wife. Dougill was a very jealous man, and has been ever since his marriage.

A trial date was set for Thursday 13th December at the West Riding Assizes in Leeds. Mr Horace Marshall and Mr Lowenthal KC appeared for the prosecution.

Evidence was given by William Storey and by the victim's sister who recounted the awful events of the fateful night. The prisoner's past behaviour and mental state were presented as evidence. William Storey attested to James Dougill's 'chronic alcoholism and jealousy'. Dougill had apparently, on more than one occasion, 'threatened to take out his wife's heart and hang it around her neck!' Another neighbour testified to overhearing Dougill say to his wife, 'I will make you fit for no one to look at.'

Since the night of the murder Dougill had been held on remand at Wakefield Jail and the resident prison doctor at the jail, Dr Bevan Lewis, was called and asked

to give evidence regarding the prisoner's mental state.
He considered Dougill, 'to be insane and ought to have
been in an asylum years ago.' Dougill's daughter Susannah
testified that her father suffered from Delirium Tremens,
also known as the 'DTs', a condition caused by withdrawal
from alcohol, bringing about an onset of confusion,
usually three days into the withdrawal symptoms and
lasting for further two to three days. The physical effects
included shaking, shivering, irregular heart rate, and
sweating.

Unsurprisingly, the jury found James Dougill 'not guilty of
the act of murder but guilty of the act of killing his wife',
although they believed him to be insane at the time of the
killing. The judge, Mr Justice Bigham, announced to the
court, 'James Luther Dougill, you have been found guilty
of the act of killing your wife, although the circumstances
of your state of mind means you will be detained
indefinitely during His Majesty's pleasure.' As Dougill was
escorted from the court by two burly police officers, his
seven-year-old son rushed forward, grabbed his father's
hand, and said, 'Goodbye, dad'.

James Dougill was considered an extreme threat to
himself and others and was transferred to Broadmoor
Criminal Lunatic Asylum Hospital as it was then known,
at Crowthorne in Berkshire. The hospital at Broadmoor
was, in 1906 as it is now, a high security facility. James
Dougill would never be released from Broadmoor and
he would never see any of his seven children again.
He spent a further 32 years detained at His Majesty's

pleasure, although 'His Majesty' had changed four times since Dougill's initial incarceration. His release was never deemed safe or appropriate and he eventually passed away of 'senile decay' in November 1938 at the age of 76, just as Adolf Hitler had announced to the worried world a speeding up of the rearmament of the German Army.

Inspector Fairburn was commended on his bravery and resourcefulness. He would soon be promoted to Superintendent.

Returning to 1906, there is a rather sad and poignant footnote to the tragic story. Catherine Dougill was buried in Pateley Bridge and a large gathering mourned at her graveside. Following her death, and the incarceration of James Dougill, the seven children were looked after, as best they could, by neighbours and relatives. However, the Relieving Officer for the Pateley Bridge Board of Guardians called on the children in December 1906 (five months after their mother's death) and found them in a 'destitute condition'. A small sum of money left by a relative for their care had long since been exhausted. The Board of Guardians granted a relief amount to help care for the children, while an attempt was made to find suitable homes for them. The children ranged in age from 15 to just a few months old.

William Storey, the children's uncle, adopted one of the boys, his namesake William. Rev Rogerson, the Vicar of St Cuthbert's in Pateley Bridge, placed three more of the children under the care of the Waifs and Strays Society. He also tried to find homes for the remaining three, although there does not seem to be any record of his success in achieving this.

Susannah, the brave 15-year-old daughter who was present at the time of her mother's murder, and who had courageously given evidence in court against her father, married a young man, Thomas Hargrave, in Leeds in 1912, at the age of 22. It can only be hoped that she managed to rekindle a happy adult life for herself from the ashes of her childhood.

THE BATMAN AND THE MAJOR

On the quaintly named Penny Pot Lane, a quiet back road leading from Harrogate into the Dales, lies the Hildebrand Army Barracks. Named after General Arthur BR Hildebrand, the camp began life as a tented base during the Great War. Following that, it has served as a training camp for the Royal Artillery, general hospital for the US Army and an Army Apprentices' School. It is currently the site of the Army Technical Training College. During 1955, although the US Army no longer used the site, it still maintained a large medical reception centre. In addition to doctors and orderlies, a large number of female staff were employed as nurses.

Soldiers from the 9th Regiment of the Queen's Own Lancers, also based at the barracks, could often be found drinking in the pubs of Harrogate and the surrounding villages, perhaps discussing National Service, the recent hanging of Ruth Ellis, or perhaps persuading a nurse to cuddle up in the back row of the Gaumont Picture House while the latest horror film, *The Quatermass Experiment*, flickered on the big screen.

One female officer at the camp was not
'off base' on Tuesday 29th November 1955.
Major Grace Margaret Hogg was a hard-
working member of the medical team at
the barracks. Aged 50, she was unmarried
and had dedicated her life to the army.
After serving with the Red Cross during
the Second World War she had joined the
Queen Alexandra's Royal Nursing Corps.

Awarded the honorary rank of Major, as reward for her
devotion to duty, she had finished yet another long shift
as Matron at the base's medical centre and was returning
to her quarters in 'Igloo' barracks. It was now late on
Tuesday evening. The night was dark, she had worked a
long shift, so she closed the curtains, put on her nightdress
and got into bed. Just as she began to drift off to sleep she
was startled by a knocking at the door. Slightly annoyed,
she pulled back the covers, got out of bed and switched
on the light. She enquired, 'who is it?', but there was no
answer, so she opened the door. There was a young man
in uniform stood in the doorway. She recognised him
instantly.

'What are you doing here?', she demanded to know.

'I have been drinking', the young man replied.

'Well, you had better get back to bed and see the Mess
Sergeant in the morning!'

Suddenly the man, who had seemed calm until that
moment, snapped. He rushed forward and grabbed Grace
Hogg by the throat. Not letting go, he swung her around,

and onto the bed. He didn't loosen his stranglehold, not even for an instant, and came crashing down on top of her. His vice-like grip coupled with the weight of his body on top of her, meant she could not struggle free. He squeezed harder and harder, pushing deeper into her neck, until his thumbs became swollen and red. Within minutes she had stopped moving. Thinking she was dead, he removed his hands. But he did not panic and rush out of the room. Instead, he remained, emotionlessly evaluating his next move.

The following morning, Wednesday 30th November 1955, around 8.30am, Major Grace Hogg was expected at the Officers' Mess for breakfast. She had always been punctual and reliable, so her fellow officers were somewhat surprised. They waited for a few minutes, but when she still failed to arrive, two of her colleagues decided to go and knock on the door of her quarters. Perhaps she was ill, or had overslept, they thought to themselves. The officers found her door locked. They knocked, but there was no answer.

Grace Hogg had an orderly assigned to her, known in the army as a 'batman'. Major Hogg's orderly was a young lancer with the 9th Regiment by the name of Private Leslie Edwards. One of his duties was to bring Major Hogg her morning cup of tea at 7.30am precisely. The officers decided to check Private Edwards' quarters, to see if he had remembered to do so, but he was not in his room either. A call was sent out, but he could not be located anywhere on the base. In his possession, given to him as part of his duties, was the only other key to Grace Hogg's room.

Another nurse, who was quartered in the same barracks as Grace Hogg, did remember seeing Private Edwards taking a cup of tea to Grace Hogg's room as 7.30am that morning. He had knocked and entered. She thought little of it, as it was his normal morning routine. That was the last time anyone has seen Edwards. He did not appear to be anywhere on the base either.

The officers decided to force an entry into Grace Hogg's quarters. They pushed their shoulders heavily against the door until the lock gave way. Not knowing what to expect inside, they were relieved, if not slightly perplexed, to find the room tidy, clean, and undisturbed. The bed was made, and there was no sign of a robbery or a struggle. Even the cup of tea, brought that morning by Private Edwards, was still sat on the bedside cabinet. It was undrunk and cold. Grace Hogg's colleagues decided to search the room for a clue as to her whereabouts. They opened the drawers and the bedside cabinet, which seemed to offer no clues. However, the wardrobe was securely locked. Despite trying to force the lock, her colleagues could not open it, so decided to call the Harrogate Police.

On their arrival the police were quickly informed of the puzzling circumstances and decided to force open the wardrobe door. Inside, at the bottom of the wardrobe, was the body of Grace Hogg. She was still in her nightdress, which was heavily bloodstained. Her head had been covered with a brown dress, presumably taken from the wardrobe, and around her neck one of her silk stockings had been tightly tied. There were some cuts and bruises to the body although her hands were unmarked, probably meaning she had been attacked so quickly that she had not had time to defend herself.

Police suspicions immediately centred on the missing batman. A full description was issued to local police stations and nearby police forces, 'Private Leslie Edwards, age 24, probably in uniform, around 5' 8" in height, medium build, with short brown hair. Wearing a wedding band'.

Meanwhile, the police ordered an autopsy on the victim and detectives attempted to figure out the motive for such a savage and unprovoked attack. Grace Hogg was known to be a spinster, there were no jealous lovers or a husband to consider. She was rumoured to be well off financially, so robbery was perhaps a motive. Her purse and handbag were still in her room. There was no jewellery, although her colleagues said she seldom wore any. It was also noticed that her watch was missing, which she had been seen wearing the previous evening during her shift.

A witness reported seeing a man in uniform boarding a bus from Harrogate bus station early on that Wednesday morning, although the witness could not remember where the bus had been heading. It was a beginning; although the man, if indeed it was Private Edwards, could have been travelling anywhere in the country.

The police busied themselves in the hunt for Edwards. However, they would not have to wait long to apprehend their chief suspect. Later that same evening, the Liverpool police received a phone call from a public callbox in the city, 'My name is Edwards, Leslie Edwards. I want to give myself up.' He was promptly met by officers from the Liverpool police who cautioned him and arranged his transportation back to Harrogate. Edwards was handed into custody at Harrogate Police Station the following morning, to be met by Detective Inspector Gledhill of the Yorkshire Police.

'Leslie Edwards, I am arresting you on suspicion of the murder of Grace Margaret Hogg on the night of 29th November 1955, or the early morning of 30th November. Do you wish to say anything?'

'I suppose I ought to say I'm sorry, but I cannot.'

Edwards was questioned by Detective Inspector Gledhill. However, any thoughts that he would refuse to co-operate with the investigation were short-lived. He immediately informed the police that he would like to make a full confession.

An initial arraignment hearing was arranged at Knaresborough Magistrates' Court and the police, armed with Edwards' statement, were confident that they possessed enough evidence for the case to be sent to trial. Mr MD Hutchison QC, appearing for the Crown at the arraignment, read the text from Edwards' confession to the court:

After my arrest I told the police that I had been assigned as batman for two women at the barracks, Miss Hogg and another called Miss Ward. I asked to be taken off that duty. The reason was that frequently it had come into my mind to strangle someone. I was drinking on Tuesday night in Harrogate. When I was walking back it came into my mind again about strangling Miss

*Hogg. When I reached the barracks I decided to rob Major Hogg's
quarters instead. The reason I wanted to do this was because I
wanted to go to prison and I knew that if I was in prison I would
be out of harm's way and would not strangle Miss Hogg or Miss
Ward. When I entered Miss Hogg's quarters it was in darkness.
The lights went on and Major Hogg came to the front door. She
said: "What are you doing here?" I said: "I have been drinking".
She said: "You had better get back to bed and see the Mess
Sergeant In the morning".*

*Then something snapped in my head. I got hold of her by the
throat and pushed her back into the bedroom and on to the bed.
I pressed on her throat so hard that my right thumb is badly
swollen. After a time I thought she was dead, so I took my hands
from her throat. I then got hold of her stocking and tied it round
her throat very tight. Before I tied the stocking round her throat I
was intimate with her. I then sat on the floor of the bedroom and
started to think, and realised what I had done. My father always
said that I would meet a bad end and that came into my mind
then. I had a look to see if she was dead, and when I found out
she was, I looked round for some money. I found £5 in notes and
a lot of 3d. pieces —about 9 shillings worth. I took the watch off
her wrist and kept it. That is all I got. I tidied the bed a bit and
pushed Major Hogg's body onto the floor. I then put her body in
the cupboard and locked the door. I then went back to my quarters
and went to sleep.*

*Next morning as usual, about 7.30 am, I made a cup of tea and
took it to her in her quarters. Then I left the barracks and went
to Harrogate. I got a bus to Leeds, then a train. When I got to
Liverpool, I went to the pictures and had some drinks. I knew It
would be in the papers, so I bought one this morning and decided
to give myself up.*

The next witness to be called at the hearing, Miss Barbara Harper, of Royal Crescent in Harrogate, testified that she had seen Edwards in a public house on the evening of 29th November, 'He told me he had had eight pints of beer already that evening. He had two more pints of beer while he was with my party. Then later, Edwards walked home with me, and we stayed talking for five minutes'.

Professor CJ Polson, head of the Department of Forensic Medicine at Leeds University, was called to testify as a medical expert:

In my opinion the cause of death was asphyxia and shock, due to strangulation, and this was accompanied by certain other injuries. There were no injuries to her hands to suggest that she defended herself against an attack, probably meaning the attack was too sudden, or a complete surprise. The probable sequence of events was manual strangulation, which caused unconsciousness, followed by sexual interference of a particularly violent nature, and finally strangulation with the silk stocking.

When asked to speak, Edwards looked up at the magistrates and replied, 'I have nothing to say'.

A Crown Court trial date was set for Thursday 8th March 1956 at the Assizes in Leeds. In the intervening time the magistrates ordered a full psychological assessment of the prisoner.

The trial opened on the morning of 8th March. However, it was to be a short hearing – one of the shortest murder trials in British legal history. Mr Justice Donovan took evidence from just one witness, Dr JL Walker the Chief Medical Officer at Armley Jail in Leeds. The doctor stated to the court that he had:

*Kept Leslie Edwards until close observation during his two-month
period on remand and I have conducted several interviews
with the prisoner. He has been suffering from schizophrenia and
mass auditory hallucinations, and thought he had heard a voice
ordering him to kill Major Hogg for some three months before the
actual crime. Edwards told me that it was his original idea to rob
Major Hogg and then give himself up. He thought that, in this
way, he would be able to avoid the orders of the voices in his head
by going to prison. The prisoner, was discharged from the Army
in 1950 with a psychopathic personality disorder and emotional
abnormalities, that showed features of schizophrenia. In 1950
he had also attempted to commit suicide. In 1953 he re-joined
the Army, saying nothing about his previous service (which was
somehow overlooked during the recruitment process), and this
time his Army character was assessed as "very good".*

*When discussing details of the offence generally, Edwards has
displayed an extreme nonchalance; even when it came to the
most gruesome details in the depositions. He has expressed a
high regard for Major Hogg, but has said he is not at all sorry
for having caused her death. He was not at all worried about the
possible consequences, and found the court proceedings "funny"
and "interesting".*

*Edwards has spoken of a voice driving him harder and harder;
and told me the voice constantly ordered him to kill Major Hogg.
Although he knew that he was doing wrong, he was so influenced
by the voice in his head that his powers of self-control were greatly
reduced. He had been clinically insane for some time before the
attack. It is my opinion that he is unfit to plead, and not of
sufficient intelligence to follow the details of his trial.*

After speaking for ten minutes Dr Walker stood down. Following legal consultation, Mr Justice Donovan ordered that Edwards was not fit to stand trial and he ordered that the prisoner be detained 'until Her Majesty's pleasure be known'.

Leslie Edwards was taken from the court and confined in a secure hospital for the rest of his life, leaving his young wife to pick up the pieces of her shattered existence.

Grace Hogg was buried in Harrogate and given full military honours. Following her death she left a large sum of money to her family (today's equivalent of £150,000), perhaps justifying the police's initial belief that robbery had been the motive for her attack. However, many other questions remain unanswered. Why had Edwards been allowed to re-enlist in the army? How was a man with a diagnosed psychopathic personality disorder permitted to act as batman to two female officers?

With these, and other, questions in mind I contacted the National Archives in London to obtain a copy of Leslie Edwards' records. To my disappointment I discovered that all information relating to the case has been sealed, under the terms of the '75-year rule'; and will not be made available to the general public until 1st January 2032, at the earliest. I attempted to file a request under the Freedom of Information Act 2000, however this was also refused. Apparently, I was not the first to try. It seems it is not yet in the public interest to uncover the full story behind the death of Grace Margaret Hogg.

SYMPATHY FOR A MURDERER

There is, perhaps, no crime of murder that better sums up the hopelessness and squalid struggle of daily life for the poorer classes in Victorian England, than the murder of Margaret Blades in Skipton on the night of the 1st-2nd May 1880.

William Gladstone had recently succeeded Benjamin Disraeli as Prime Minister, Britain was just about to adopt Greenwich Mean Time, and the first cricket Test Match was played in England. Life for half of Britain's population was a constant struggle between poverty, poor working and living conditions, the threat of sickness, and overcrowding. There was very little in the way of affordable entertainment either, apart from the temporary relief offered by alcohol. There was however a lurid fascination offered by the grizzly stories of murder that filled the newspapers on an almost daily basis. In many ways, murderers became the most famous celebrities of the time. It was common for court houses and the streets outside police stations to be packed with those eager to catch a glimpse of a killer. These cold-hearted killers were often vilified for their wrongdoing and polite Victorian 'society' firmly believed in the existence of a criminal underclass. Hardly ever would a murderer be sympathised with. Except, that is, in the case of Henry Blades.

The population of Skipton was following, with garish fascination, the story that unfolded at the lodgings of Henry and Margaret Blades in Russell Street, Skipton, during the summer of 1880. Henry Blades had married Margaret in 1862, when they were both just 17-years-old. He had found employment as a leather currier and the family had recently moved into a small 'two up, two down' terraced house in Russell Street. So recently, in fact, that some of their furniture had not yet arrived and the family were having to sleep on mattresses on the floor. This seems to be symbolic of their chaotic lifestyle. The couple had four children, Thomas (15), Alfred (13), Elizabeth (11), and Arthur (9). Despite their children, it seems that the marriage was not a happy one. Both Henry and Margaret drank heavily and regularly frequented local public houses. Although, it appears, they did not do this together. Margaret was happy to socialise with groups of men, provided that they purchased her generous amounts of alcohol. This was a cause of frequent arguments between the couple, in which Henry would become increasingly jealous and enraged.

Margaret Blades had regularly complained to the police about her husband's physical assaults and intolerable behaviour towards her. This had resulted in magistrates granting her a judicial separation one year earlier (a rare occurrence in the male dominated legal system of Victorian England). Not only was Henry Blades infuriated by the magistrate's decision, he was also ordered to pay his wife an allowance of eight shillings a week (the equivalent of £50 today) towards the upkeep of the children – a sizeable amount for a working man in 1879. Nevertheless, despite the judicial separation order, the couple seemed to have resolved their differences by 1880, at which point they were living together again. Their habits do not seem to have changed, however. Henry Blades had frequently been overheard saying, 'if she gets drunk again, I'll finish her!', and 'If I had money for a razor, I'd buy one and cut her throat!'. On the afternoon of 1st May, Margaret had left the house to frequent a string of public houses in the town. Again, the couple were not together. Witnesses would later report that they were both seen 'drinking freely', but separately. The children had been left at home in the care of Thomas, the eldest son. There was no coal in the house for the fire, and only bread, dripping and sugar in the cupboard.

Henry was first to return home, around 11pm, and was furious to find that his wife was still out. He told the children that he was going to find her if it was the last thing he did. He slammed the door as he left, passing a neighbour in the street, and saying to him, 'I'll murder her this time', and 'I'll do for her before I sleep'.

After searching several public houses, including The
Star Inn and The Albion Inn, then walking the length of
Sackville Street and Mill Lane, he was unable to find her
and returned home, with the seething anger growing
inside him. However, when he opened his front door, he
was told by his eldest son that their mother had returned
home during his absence and had already gone to bed.
With the children safely in their bedroom Henry went into
his wife's room and slammed the door shut. 'Where have
you been all the day?', he demanded to know. She replied,
'Not with thee'.

The children, whose bedroom was just across the landing,
heard a dull thud, as if someone had been hit by a heavy
object, then a scream, followed by what was later described
as a 'murmuring' noise. Terrified, they did not dare leave
their bedroom.

The following morning the children got out of bed at
about 8am. As they opened the bedroom door, their father
was already stood on the landing outside. He motioned
them to all go straight downstairs and waited until they
had done so.

Elizabeth asked, 'I want to go and see mother'. Her father
refused, instead telling her, 'your mother is so poorly
she could not bear anyone bothering with her'. Elizabeth
inquired, 'Is she dead?' 'What are you talking that silly talk
for?', her father replied.

Later, Henry Blades took a tray of dinner upstairs to his
wife. The children had remained downstairs all day, having

been told not to disturb their mother for any reason. However, after being upstairs for ten minutes, Henry brought the uneaten tray of food downstairs again, and went into the back-kitchen. Thinking he was out of sight of the children, he hurriedly ate the plateful himself. He then carried the plate through into the other room and told the children, 'she has eaten her dinner.'

Henry Blades then returned to the back-kitchen, fetched a length of bed cord, and began to fashion a section of rope from it using a knife. He slung the cut portion over a hook in the ceiling. Hearing the movement, one of the children came into the room and asked him, 'what are you doing that for?' He replied, 'to hang something up.' He had been writing something on a slate. His daughter grabbed it and tried to read it; but her father snatched it back before she was able to.

It was now 7pm and Henry Blades ordered the children to go outside and play. Under protest they were turned out of the house and he locked the door behind them. He had intended to take his own life, but it seems that he changed his mind. The children, unable to get back in, walked to their aunt's house; which was nearby. Once there, and clearly disturbed, their aunt asked them what was wrong. They replied, 'we think mother is dead.' Aunt Lizzie immediately told the children she would return to their house with them. On returning home the children told their father, 'Aunt Lizzie is coming'. Henry Blades immediately left the house. He did not intend to be there when his wife's sister arrived.

The children's aunt Lizzie Chester, together with another neighbour, Ellen Dawson, went into the Blades' house. It was now 8.45pm. The two women rushed up the narrow stairs to the bedroom at the front of the house. Quickly pulling back the curtains of the darkened room, they noticed the bed covers had been pulled right up. It was obvious that someone was lying underneath; and the two women hastily pulled the covers back, saying, 'Margaret, Margaret'. They were greeted with the pallid, lifeless body of Margaret Blades. They initially recoiled in horror; but were able to gather their composure and sent for the police and Doctor Wylie.

An immediate manhunt was launched for Henry Blades who, in the midst of the dramatic discovery, had slipped away. Police officers searched back yards, outbuildings and alleyways in the town, all to no avail. Finally, 24 hours later, while searching outbuildings, he was found hiding in a hayloft, at Bradley, about a mile outside of Skipton. He appeared to have been heading in the direction of Rombald's Moor. Henry Blades was immediately arrested. He initially gave a false name, 'William Smith from Keighley'; but later admitted he was Henry Blades. Sergeant Chisholm escorted Blades back to Skipton Police Station where he was charged with his wife's wilful murder, to which he replied, 'it was no wilful murder'. An enormous crowd gathered outside, all anxious for a glimpse of the alleged murderer of Margaret Blades. Blades was then remanded at Armley Jail in Leeds, while investigations were undertaken.

Meanwhile, it seemed that public sympathy in Skipton was surprisingly tilted towards Henry Blades and not with his victim. He was described as a god-fearing, decent and hard-working young man, by all who knew him. 'Well-liked and always smartly dressed', his acquaintances said, 'who only recently had been driven to alcohol, caused by the trouble with his wife, on account of her intemperance and unfaithfulness'. It was claimed that he had become addicted to drink only as all his efforts to save his family had failed. His wife had humiliated him regularly and he could stand it no longer.

In front of the Magistrates' Bench at Skipton Town Hall on Saturday 8th May 1880 he pleaded not guilty to her murder. Blades was then hurried into a waiting police wagon to be taken to the railway station. A huge crowd had gathered, many cheering, as they jostled to obtain a better view of the prisoner. The police formed a cordon and were forced to pull down the blinds on the window of the carriage conveying him to the station, to prevent well-wishers from surging forward to push themselves against the glass, in their anxiety to wish him 'good luck'. The *Leeds Mercury* seemed to be rooting for the arrested man too, describing him as, 'about 35 years of age, with bright blue eyes and a frank and pleasant countenance. His appearance was not at all inconsistent with the character which is given him by his acquaintances. He seemed to be very cheerful and the sight of his supporters greatly improved his health and spirits.'

A trial date was set for Monday 2nd August at the Yorkshire

Summer Assizes, held at Leeds Crown Court. Mr Justice Brown oversaw the proceeding. The sympathy felt in the town for Henry Blades resulted in a considerable sum being raised for his defence. Enough, in fact, to afford the services of Mr Henry Tindal Atkinson, probably Britain's most prominent barrister at that time. Tindal Atkinson would eventually be appointed one of the country's leading judges, and his son would become Director of Public Prosecutions.

Henry Blades again pleaded not guilty to the murder of his wife and the trial commenced.

First to give evidence was Dr Wylie, who been called to Russell Street on the Sunday evening. He was able to confirm that Margaret Blades had been:

Lying on her back and appeared to have been dead for a considerable period of time. The pillows were stained with blood and on the left side of her neck was a deep ecchymosed (heavily bruised) cut, four inches long, and extending as far as the windpipe. I noticed no other stains on the neck apart from "after-death" stains, called post-mortem stains. I also found a large ecchymosed mark on the lower angle of the right shoulder blade. It resembled the front part of the sole of a boot. There was a similar but smaller mark on the right hip. I found no traces of alcohol or food in the stomach.

'In your opinion, what was the cause of death, Dr Wylie?'

Dr Wylie replied, 'Strangulation'

In cross-examination for the defence, Mr Tindal Atkinson attempted to create some doubt regarding the cause of death, alluding to Mrs Blades' poor state of health due to her excessive alcohol consumption, 'might not death have been caused by a momentary stoppage of circulation in a subject suffering from fatty degeneration of the heart?'

'I should hardly say so', replied Dr Wylie.

Tindall Atkinson pressed, 'But it is possible?'

Dr Wylie replied, 'Yes.'

'Very well, we come to the question of the rope. If it had, indeed, been done by the rope (which was shown to the court), would you not have expected to have found marks on the other parts of the neck?'

'It depends upon where the rope was placed. It (her neck) might not come in contact with the rope all round the neck.'

The rope found at the house was shown to the Doctor, 'Could this rope have produced such a mark?'

'No'

'So, if the woman had been throttled instead, would you have expected to find marks on both sides of the neck?'

'I would'.

'Supposing then, doctor, if this woman had been seized by the throat, and supposing in her struggles the man who had seized her fell upon her with his hand upon her larynx, could this have caused the strangulation to be accidental?'

'It depends how', replied the doctor, 'I don't think it would kill on the spot.'

Despite Mr Tindal Atkinson's best efforts to create some doubt in the mind of the jury, the evidence of the neighbours and the Blades' daughter Elizabeth would prove extremely damaging to Henry Blades' defence. Patience Pullen, who occupied the house next door in Russell Street, had been sitting by the hearth when she saw Margaret Blades enter her house, around 11.30pm. Sometime afterwards she heard a commotion from the Blades' bedroom. A thud, followed by a groan, then a child's scream. She also testified to hearing Elizabeth, the daughter, scream, 'Oh, father, don't!'. Her father replied, 'If you don't make less of a noise, I'll kill you.'

After the evidence of several witnesses the defence began their case. They attempted to paint Mrs Blades as a fallen woman, emphasising the point that she often referred to herself by a different name, Sarah, when drinking in the public houses of Skipton. 'Why would a woman do this, unless to prevent talk finding its way back to her husband?', Mr Tindall Atkinson asked the jury. Lizzie Fagan, a neighbour and friend of Margaret Blades, attested to the fact that the victim had been drinking in Sackville Street on the night of the murder. In addition, soldiers from the local Artillery Regiment had been in town drinking that evening, and the suggestion was made by Mr Tindal Atkinson that she may have spent some time with them.

The fact that she had spent an entire night away from home one week before the crime was also entered into evidence by the defence, as they tried to present Margaret Blades as a woman of loose morals. Another witness testified to having found Mrs Blades asleep in a field during the previous summer.

Henry Blades' version of events was also presented. An argument had developed over her long absence and the money she had spent that day:

I made to look in her dress pocket, she tried to hit me with a brass candlestick. I grabbed her and my passion getting the better of me I seized her by the side of her neck and we struggled for some time. Before I left off, we both fell on to the bed which was on the ground,

and I fell on to her side with my knee. She fell sick and was so for a while. Sometime in the early morning she gave over breathing.

Perhaps the most poignant evidence given during the trial was that of Police Sergeant Collins, who had entered the premises with Dr Wylie on that fateful Sunday evening. During the time that the doctor had been examining the body, the police officer had found the slate and an envelope on which Henry Blades had written the following:

Dear Friends – I do hope you will never let my poor children go to the workhouse, for they will do someone some good one day. No finer children born in the world than they for working. So I hope to the Lord you will do your best to them, and I think they will do the same to you. It is heartbreaking to leave them, but we must part, so I hope it will be a warning to you not to get the same fate as this. They are standing over me as I am writing. So, I will say no more, for my heart is bursting to see them.

And on a crumpled envelope which was found in the back kitchen of Russell Street:

I cannot live any longer the way things is going on, so I will bid you all goodbye, hoping to live in peace, for it has been a troublesome life, and I hope all my friends will look over it. So, I remain your sorrowful best. Goodbye to all.

(The original notes had been poorly written and badly misspelt; but are corrected here for the reader's convenience).

In summing up, Mr Justice Brown reminded the jury of their obligation to consider whether the crime was deliberate and wilful murder, or manslaughter. After just fifteen minutes they returned with a verdict of manslaughter. In passing sentence, Mr Justice Brown spoke directly to the prisoner:

Prisoner at the bar, your sentence is going to be a terrible one. You have been found guilty of a most brutal crime. The jury have taken a merciful view, and I have no doubt, a right view of the case. But you have been guilty of unmanly, wicked violence towards your wife. The sentence of this court is that you be kept in penal servitude for 20 years.

Henry Blades was led from the court a broken man and transferred to Parkhurst Prison on the Isle of Wight. He served 15 years of his 20 years' sentence and was released in October 1895. He returned to Skipton, although whether he saw his children again is not known. After managing to find employment in a leather factory, he married a cotton weaver named Priscilla in 1901 and settled in a house in Airebank Terrace. He was then 56. she was 16 years his junior. He died in 1911 at the age of 66.

It appears that at least two of Henry Blades' children were sent to work in the local mills. Young Alfred, 13 at the time of his mother's death, was already employed at one. Elizabeth, who appears to have borne the burden of witnessing the events and of having to testify in court, married a farmer in the 1890s and raised two children of her own. She seems to have displayed remarkable courage and maturity throughout the nightmarish events of that summer.

SEVENTEEN DAYS OF TERROR

On Thursday 17th June 1982, the sun rose at Norwood Edge, a beauty spot in Stainburn Forest in the Yorkshire Dales, just a few miles from the market town of Otley. The early morning dew glistened on the grass as the first warming rays cast their shadows. A solitary green car sat in a corner of the Warren picnic site car park. Its occupant was sound asleep in the driver's seat.

Police Constable David Haigh, a 29-year-old West Yorkshire Police officer, woke early that morning as his shift commenced at 6am. His alarm sounded and he quickly threw back the sheets and jumped out of bed. He listened to the news on the radio as he got ready for work. The new 20 pence coin had just been introduced and British soldiers had arrived at Port Stanley in the Falklands to receive the surrender of the Argentinian forces.

PC Haigh's first task that morning at the police station was to read the daily crime reports, in order that he could follow-up any outstanding actions recorded by the previous nightshift. First on the 'overnights' was the serving of a court summons to a suspected poacher, who had been reported as living rough and sleeping in an old van, in the Norwood Edge area of the Dales.

PC Haigh set off to issue the summons, which was a routine matter, meaning he was expected to return to patrol relatively quickly afterwards. However, when he failed to respond to several radio messages later that morning, another patrol car was dispatched to investigate, the assumption being his radio had malfunctioned or, perhaps, he had suffered an accident.

The police car approached the Warren picnic site around 8am. Through the lush, green trees, they spotted PC Haigh's lone panda car parked at the site. The distinctive black and white pattern on the side of the patrol cars, which predated the red stripe now seen on police vehicles, had earned them the nickname panda cars.

The driver's door was wide open. Apart from that, nothing seemed out of place and the car park was empty. The officers got out of their patrol car and walked around to the far side of PC Haigh's car, where they made a dreadful discovery.

PC Haigh's lifeless body lay slumped on the ground beside the open door of his patrol car, a hole from a .22 calibre bullet clearly visible in his forehead. A trickle of blood emanated from the wound. Lying on the ground, just out of reach of his outstretched right hand, was his clipboard. On it, PC Haigh had written in block capitals: 'CLIVE JONES. DOB: 18:10:44, LEEDS NFA. KYF 326P'. This gave his colleagues their first vital clue.

The registration number was quickly traced to a metallic green Citroen car which had been purchased for £475 in London, six months earlier. The previous owner, a Mr Clive Jones, was able to describe selling the car to, 'a dark-haired, well dressed northerner who gave his name as RD Carlisle, and that he told me he had just come back from working on the oil rigs'. Mr Clive Jones, it appeared, had sold the car six months earlier and the new owner had not updated the vehicle's logbook. It seemed likely that the occupant of the car had given PC Haigh the previous owner's name when challenged by the officer in the car park. Tragically, whatever the outcome of that conversation had been, it resulted in the officer being shot and killed.

Detectives located a witness who was able to confirm seeing the green metallic Citroen parked at the Warren picnic site at 6:35am on the morning of the shooting. The witness had observed a dishevelled, unshaven, dark haired man asleep in the driver's seat.

The poacher that PC Haigh had intended to serve the summons to was quickly eliminated from the enquiry, and a nationwide search for the car was undertaken. As it appeared that the killer had been in possession of the car since purchasing it six months earlier, police theorised that many witnesses must have seen the vehicle and its owner during that period. Just two days later, the green Citroen was found abandoned in a cornfield close to the village of Ledsham, 27 miles from the scene of PC Haigh's murder. With that discovery the trail had gone cold.

Early the following morning (Sunday 20th June), 53 miles away, close to the village of Torksey in Lincolnshire,

75-year-old widow Freda Jackson thought she heard an intruder in her home and got out of bed to investigate. As she went into the next room she was confronted by an armed gunman. The intruder tied Mrs Jackson up, gagged her, and robbed her of £4.50 and a small amount of food, before hurriedly leaving through the back door. Unable to raise the alarm, Mrs Jackson remained tied up until the following morning, when a delivery driver on his rounds heard her calls for help; and called the police. Mrs Jackson was badly shaken, but otherwise unharmed. She was able to describe her assailant to the police as follows, 'About 35 to 40, slim with dark straggly hair, who looked and smelled unkempt, and who spoke with a "northern" accent'.

Three days later, on Wednesday 23rd June, in the village of Girton, near Newark and less than 9 miles from Torksey, the same man broke into a house belonging to 52-year-old electrician George Luckett and his wife Sylvia. Still armed, he easily subdued the couple and tied them together by the elbows. Intending to steal their car, he went outside to check the vehicle. However, during the few minutes he was absent the Lucketts managed to slip their bonds. Furious, and without a moment's hesitation, the gunman shot both George and Sylvia Luckett in the head at close range. George was shot first and died instantly. By a miracle Sylvia was not killed and managed to make it to a neighbouring house to raise the alarm. However, she was left with permanent brain damage as a result of the shooting and was unable to recollect the incident clearly. Following the shooting, the gunman fled in the Luckett's car, a brown Rover, registration number VAU 875S, having first robbed them of a small amount of money and food.

Thanks to North Yorkshire Police's new computerised indexing database system (implemented after the costly mistakes made during the 'Yorkshire Ripper' enquiry just 12 months previously) the crimes were officially linked the following day, the 24th June, when ballistics testing proved that the same weapon fired at the scene of the Luckett's shootings, had also been used to kill PC Haigh. Police now knew that they were looking for a cold-blooded double murderer, but still did not know the man's name or identity.

Meanwhile, while the police began to unify their enquiries across three forces, the killer had returned to Yorkshire and was about to make his next move. Dalby Forest, situated just eight miles from Scarborough and comprising more than 50 square miles of thick trees, with dense foliage and undergrowth – the perfect place to evade a police manhunt. PC Kenneth Oliver, a North Yorkshire Police dog handler was on van patrol covering the area of Dalby Forest, when he noticed a dishevelled man sat in a parked brown Rover car, registration number CYG 344T.

Remembering the circulated reports of the Luckett's stolen vehicle, and being suspicious of the man sat in the vehicle, PC Oliver readied his dog and carefully approached the vehicle. The driver's window was wound down. When he was just a few steps from the window, the man in the car fired his handgun, hitting the police officer in the face. Miraculously, he was not killed and managed to retreat towards his van. As he crawled backwards towards his patrol van, the gunman emerged from the brown Rover and fired twice more at PC Oliver. Unbelievably, the two shots grazed his scalp and arm, but did not kill him. He managed to release his barking dog and ordered it to attack the gunman, who then turned his gun on the dog. The dog was wounded but survived the shooting. This diversion gave PC Oliver valuable time to stagger to the safety of a nearby house and raise the alarm. Meanwhile, the quick-thinking gunman managed to disable the police radio in the van, then set fire to the Rover car, before disappearing into the depths of Dalby Forest.

Armed police arrived quickly on the scene and hundreds of officers were drafted in for what would become Britain's largest manhunt. The forest was surrounded as effectively as possible, although the light was now fading, and the man may have already slipped through the cordon of armed officers. For two days and nights the search of Dalby Forest continued for the killer now dubbed by the press 'The Phantom Of The Forest'. Local gamekeepers assisted the police, residents were evacuated and the forest was blanketed with an armed cordon of marksmen, with roadblocks on every road.

Somehow, mainly thanks to luck, bad weather, and his obvious outdoor survival skills, the gunman escaped. 'The Phantom of the Forest', however, would not keep the police waiting long. Two days later, on 28th June, he would strike again. Police Sergeant David Thomas Winter and PC Michael Woods were carrying out routine vehicle checks on the A64 road near the village of Old Malton, about 20 miles east from the site of PC Oliver's shooting at Norwood Edge, in case the killer was returning to the Dales in search of a hiding place. The two officers received a radio call reporting a suspicious looking man, described as 'looking like a tramp, wearing a blue woollen hat and khaki jacket, dirty and unshaven', near a public house on the outskirts of the village. As they arrived at the location they immediately noticed a man matching the description. He had a long walking stick in his right hand and a blue plastic shopping bag in his other. Sergeant Winter got out of the car and approached the man. As he did so, the man quickly pulled a handgun from his clothing and began shooting wildly at the officer. Sergeant Winter turned sharply and fled along a nearby alley, then threw himself over a low stone wall for cover, but the gunman gave chase and cornered the officer, shooting him three times at point-blank range, twice in the torso, once in the neck. He was killed instantly. The gunman then escaped, again into a thickly wooded forest nearby, whilst PC Woods frantically raised the alarm on the police radio.

Again, the area was immediately surrounded by police, many of them armed, and a thorough sweep undertaken. All houses, shops and business premises were searched, and the villages of Malton and Old Malton were effectively sealed off, with all roads blocked. Yet, somehow, 'The Phantom' evaded capture. Luck was on his side once again, as a torrential downpour hindered the police dog search, making it impossible to pick up a scent. By the following morning more than 600 officers were involved in hunting for 'The Phantom' – with one in six of them armed, and each officer involved in the hunt wearing protective body armour. Police helicopters were used; with thermal imaging and infra-red cameras deployed in the hunt. Yet the triple murderer was still nowhere to be found. Tensions were running high among the officers involved in the manhunt. The gunman obviously had a hatred of the police – were they hunting him, or was he hunting them?

Finally, however, the beleaguered police force was able to identify the killer; now Britain's most wanted man. On the 28th June, a police constable from the Warrant department of West Yorkshire Police discovered that a man named Barry Peter Prudom had failed to answer court bail following a serious assault in Leeds in January 1982. The eagle-eyed officer noticed that Prudom's date of birth was recorded as 18th October 1944 – the same date as PC Haigh had written on his clipboard at the Warren picnic site in the Dales, shortly before he was killed. Because of the close proximity of the attack in Leeds and the date of birth written on the clipboard, a photograph of Prudom was shown to PC Kenneth Oliver, the officer who had been injured in the Dalby Forest shooting. PC Oliver unhesitatingly identified Prudom as the man who had shot him. Prudom's fingerprints were also matched to those taken from the abandoned green Citroen car. Police now knew beyond any doubt the identity of 'The Phantom Of The Forest'. An artist's impression of Prudom was issued to the press and public; with the warning that he was wanted for questioning in connection with three murders, and was likely armed and extremely dangerous.

'Wanted' posters were placed all across Yorkshire and an expert Army tracker and survival expert, Eddie McGee, was drafted in to assist the search. He managed to locate a 'hide' that Prudom had constructed in Dalby Forest, but despite following a trail left by Prudom, he once again escaped. McGee was of the opinion, however, that Prudom was nearing exhaustion and they would locate him sooner rather than later.

At 5.45am on the morning of 4th July, the police received a telephone call from a Mr Maurice Johnson of East Mount, Malton. Mr Johnson told the investigating officers that he, his wife, and son had been held hostage at gunpoint by Prudom since 5pm the previous afternoon. Prudom had not harmed any of them, but he had tied them up. During the time they had been held hostage, Prudom had confessed to them the murders of PC Haigh, Mr Luckett, and Sergeant Winter, and the attempted murders of Mrs Luckett and PC Oliver. He then vanished from the Johnson's home under cover of darkness around 5am the following morning. The Johnsons then waited for a safe period of time to elapse before contacting the police, in case Prudom was still watching the house.

The area was immediately surrounded and the village sealed off. Within two hours Eddie McGee and an armed escort located fresh footprints running across the grounds of the nearby Malton tennis and bowling club. The footprints terminated by a pile of old fencing panels stacked against a stone wall, which were covered with brambles and bracken. McGee, noticing that some of the bracken had been disturbed, began to probe the undergrowth with a long stick. He caught a glimpse of a blue plastic bag, and immediately knew he had located Prudom's hiding place.

Armed police surrounded the area and shouted to Prudom to surrender – but there was no answer. Chief Inspector David Clarkson of West Yorkshire Police, and Inspector Brian Cheton of North Yorkshire Police – both armed officers – approached the fencing panels and attempted to move them away from the wall. Prudom fired a shot from behind the fencing panels, and both officers were forced to move back. Police officers fired four shotgun rounds in retaliation. Further calls to surrender were again met by stony silence, so the order was given for further shots to be fired and for percussion grenades to be thrown, in an attempt to disorientate Prudom. The officers then returned and again attempted to remove the fencing panel. This time they were successful. Beneath the panel, Barry Prudom lay dead, with a pistol on his chest pointing upwards.

The 17-day manhunt, which in total had involved 4,293 officers from 12 different police forces, was over.

But why had Barry Peter Prudom embarked on such a frenzied rampage? Born in 1944, he never met his father. His mother had married a man named Alex Prudom in 1949, and Barry had taken his stepfather's surname. After

an unremarkable youth in Leeds he had married in 1965.
Tiring of a normal working life, Prudom had enrolled in
the TA SAS Volunteer Regiment in Leeds. He participated
in numerous weekend camps and manoeuvres and was
described as a fitness freak; but was evaluated as mentally
unsuitable for the SAS. Bitterly disappointed, Prudom
still retained his enthusiasm for the mercenary lifestyle. A
later search of his home yielded many survivalist textbooks
– including one called 'No Need To Die' – written by a
tracker named...Eddie McGee.

In 1977, following his affair with a neighbour, Prudom's
wife Gillian had divorced him and taken the children
with her. He later met a girl called Carol Francis, who was
half his age, and the couple took up a nomadic lifestyle,
eventually travelling to Canada and the United States of
America.

It was during his time spent in the USA that Prudom
obtained the pistol that he subsequently used in his
rampage, a Beretta Model 71 Jaguar, which he had
smuggled back to the UK when the couple returned in
1981.

However, they argued repeatedly and after Barry attacked
and severely wounded a 54-year-old motorist with an iron
bar in January 1982, the offence for which he had not
answered the court summons mentioned earlier, Carol left
him and returned to live with her mother.

What triggered Prudom to kill has never been clearly
ascertained, but he was evidently unstable after Carol
ended their relationship.

During the night in which Prudom had held the Johnson family hostage he told them,

'I am going to die but I will not be the only one. There is nowhere for me to go. Thanks for everything'.

At the inquest the coroner's jury took just 18 minutes to record a verdict of suicide. Following his death, Prudom was buried in an unmarked grave in an undisclosed Leeds cemetery. The verdict of suicide closed the door on the case of Barry Peter Prudom, and the largest armed police operation in British history, involving 12 separate police forces, and resulting in 17 days of terror that gripped the nation.

THE LANGCLIFFE TRAGEDY

There are many tragedies associated with the construction of the railway line between Settle in the Yorkshire Dales and Carlisle on the border between England and Scotland. Construction began in 1869 and would take seven long years. During that time over 6,000 workers, known as 'navvies', were employed. These men lived and worked in the remotest of locations, enduring harsh weather conditions and poor working practices. Large camps were established to house the navvies. with many becoming complete townships, including post offices and schools. The men had travelled from Ireland, Scotland and from across England to work on the construction of the railway. Some even brought their whole family with them. These camps were given names such as Inkerman, Sebastapol and Jericho. The remains of one camp—Batty Green—where over 2,000 navvies lived and worked, can still be seen near Ribblehead.

Navvies, although hard working, were looked down upon by the general public. Often brutalised by their working conditions, they were continuously blamed for any crime that took place in the vicinity, although sometimes with good reason. Drunkenness, violence, fighting and theft were commonplace. In fact, alcohol was the only solace, albeit temporary, for many of the men. Many of the railway companies even built their own taverns to ensure that the money they paid the navvies went straight back in the company's coffers. Navvies were transitory and would often arrive and disappear from campsites in the dead of night. The Midland Railway Company even financed Bible readings in an attempt to counteract the effect of drunken violence in these isolated communities.

During the seven years spent toiling on the 72 miles of track, there were hundreds of deaths (some resulting from non-existent health and safety procedures, other from accidents, suicides, fighting and exposure to the extreme cold). A smallpox outbreak at the Batty Green camp killed 80 men alone. In particular, the construction of the Ribblehead (then Batty Moss) viaduct, with its 24 massive stone arches standing 104 feet above the moor, caused such loss of life that the railway company paid for an extension to the local graveyard. On average, three men perished for every mile of railway line laid. As recently as 2020 writer Sarah Lister identified 20 previously unrecorded navvy graves at the Parish Church in Settle.

There are many stories surrounding the deaths, tragedies and violence of the men who built the Settle to Carlisle Railway (literally) with their own hands. Enough for a book dedicated solely for that purpose. This chapter tells just one of them.

Ellis Parker was a native of Whalley, a small village in Lancashire. Born in 1846 he had been employed as a labourer and factory worker until, at the age of 24, he heard about the construction of the new railway. The work was back-breaking, but the pay was much better than that at the factory. As much as five shillings a day (approximately £30 today), with just a few pence deducted for their bed at one of navvy camps. At the end of a long week of toil Ellis Parker would join with a group of his fellow workers and seek out an inn or hostelry and engage in heavy drinking sessions, known in navvy parlance as 'going on a randy'.

It appears, at some point during his stint working the railway line, Ellis Parker decided to use an alias - Ellis Newton - for reasons which are not known. It may be that he had encountered some previous trouble with the authorities or had moved on from a previous employment at which he had blackened his name and wished to distance himself from it. It was common practice among the navvies, as they moved around the country looking for employment, to use a variety of different aliases or sometimes have no known name at all. Sadly, the navvy graveyards and memorials are littered with gravestones to unknown men.

On the night of Saturday 8th January 1871, Ellis and a fellow navvy, Tom, took their hard-earned pay and walked into the small village of Langcliffe, close to Settle, on the River Ribble. The night was bitterly cold and the men had no wish to return to the camp. At 9.30pm they entered The

Bay Horse, a small 'beerhouse', kept by a Mr Christopher Wright, at his home in Langcliffe. Several other navvies were already drinking on the premises and they offered Ellis Parker and Tom a drink from their large pot of ale. Unlike today, with the advent of modern licensing laws, many inns and alehouses were little more than a front room used by the homeowner to sell beer and whisky. As a consequence, they were able to supply a very affordable brew to their grateful customers. The 1830 Beerhouse Act had allowed any person to brew and sell beer directly from his home, upon the payment of a licence costing two guineas (about £250 today).

Christopher Wright was a kindly and elderly man, who had retired from a life working in the cotton mills due to the loss of his right arm. Instead, he had taken up the less physically demanding role of beer seller. In the days before National Insurance and the State Pension, work was

the only way of providing for your family, no matter your age. Now aged 76 he still earned a living selling beer to the navvies and local agricultural workers. Living in The Bay Horse with him were his wife Agnes (aged 67) and his two grand-daughters Agnes and Annie, who occasionally helped to serve in the bar.

Looking at his pocket watch, Christopher Wright noted that it was 9.30pm. He hoped the two navvies would not stay long, as he wished to retire for the night. It was noted that the men were 'fresh, but not drunk'. However, the two men gradually became louder and more boisterous. At 11pm Christopher asked the men politely to leave as he wished to close shop. There were other customers present and Mr Wright asked them to finish their drinks and leave too. Ellis Parker opened the door and motioned his fellow navvies outside; but refused to leave himself. Instead, with his drinking companion Tom, he asked for yet more drink. The two men pushed their way through the bar and entered the private part of the house. As the two navvies became more aggressive Mr Wright demanded to know what they thought they were doing. His wife, Agnes, tried a different tactic. She approached the two men and politely asked them to go, offering them sixpence each if they promised to do so. Ellis Parker agreed, swearing to leave, 'as true as God in Heaven'. He then took the sixpence, but promptly changed his mind announcing, 'I will stay all night!' He then demanded a gallon of ale, requesting that the two girls bring it to him. They refused, hoping the pair would leave, but they remained.

Around midnight, with the men still refusing to leave, Annie was sent to fetch the constable, PC Christopher Jackson. However, unbeknown to Annie, the local constable had been moved to another post in a different village, just one week previously, and Langcliffe was temporarily without a police officer. Christopher Wright's grand-daughter Agnes and her sweetheart Peter Smith (who had been waiting outside for her to finish work), instead decided to run the one mile to Settle in search of another police officer. Unfortunately, they were unable to locate one and returned empty handed. They joined Christopher Wright, his wife, and Annie in the kitchen. Agnes announced to the men and to her grandmother 'the police are coming'. Ellis shouted, 'I don't care for any bobbies. If three policemen came I'd master them all. If six policemen came I'd punch their bloody brains out'. He then demanded some supper saying that he knew Mrs Wright kept some cheese in the kitchen. Ellis Parker then bolted the door, leaving the Wrights in no doubt as to who was in control of an increasingly volatile situation. He taunted Christopher Wright, stating that he would show Wright who was the landlord of the house, proclaiming 'I am the Champion of England!' Christopher Wright protested loudly, 'I will have my door open', and attempted to pull upon the bolt. His wife followed behind him carrying a candle. Ellis Parker pushed Christopher Wright away and knocked Mrs Wright against the door-frame; inflicting a cut on her arm.

Christopher Wright again implored Parker to leave and endeavoured to pull him towards the door by the sleeve of Parker's jacket. Enraged by this, and with a face like thunder, Parker swung around and grabbed the elderly Mr Wright, throwing him aggressively onto the stone floor. Whilst the old man lay stunned on the floor, Parker punched him again and again. Mr Wright cried out in pain, 'The Lord be merciful, I'm killed'. Parker then grabbed him by his ankles and dragged him along the passageway into the lobby. He then threw Mr Wright against the stone floor again, and kicked him in the side, viciously, and at least three times with his clogs, while Wright's body lay slumped on the flagstones. Mrs Wright, terrified, ran out of the house. Her grand-daughter Agnes, bravely tried to assist her grandfather, attempting to help him into a chair. However, Ellis Parker shouted out, 'I'll dash her bloody brains out if she doesn't let him alone. Let the old bugger suffer'.

Christopher Wright, as he tried to move, cried out and complained of the pain in his back. Ellis Parker laughed, taunting him, 'he's makin' it up!', putting his arm in a mock sling and waving it in the air.

He and his companion then remained in the beer house, mocking the injured Christopher Wright and continuing drinking until 5am, when they left, presumably to sleep off the drink. Meanwhile the battered and bleeding Christopher Wright was left semi-conscious on the floor. He was helped, with great difficulty, by his terrified wife and granddaughters into his bed and Doctor Altham was sent for.

On the following day (10th January), Ellis Parker was arrested by PC William Taylor from Settle. Christopher Wright's grand-daughter Agnes had accompanied the police constable to help identify Parker. He was found, sleeping off the excesses of the previous night, in a railway hut at Willywood. It was noted that he was wearing clogs with iron rims which, assuming that they were the same pair he had been wearing on the previous evening, would have caused substantial injury. When woken by Constable Taylor, Parker firstly claimed he had been in bed asleep all night, and then admitted, 'he struck me first'.

Parker was charged 'with having committed a violent assault upon Christopher Wright, a beer seller, at Langcliffe, near Settle.' A remand hearing was called in Settle and local magistrates Mr John Birkbeck and the Rev. HJ Swale requested a report from Doctor Altham. The doctor confirmed that he had attended to Mr Wright's injuries during the early hours of the 9th January and in his opinion, 'it appeared somewhat doubtful as to whether Christopher Wright, who is in his 76th year, will recover from the injuries he has received.'

On hearing this evidence, it was decided to remand the prisoner while further enquiries were made.

Sadly, Christopher Wright died from his injuries six days later, still in the bed where his family had carried him to on the night of the attack. He never fully regained consciousness. A Coroner's Inquest was arranged for the 17th January 1871 and Ellis Parker was charged by Mr Thomas Parkinson Brown, the local Coroner, with 'having, on the 9th inst., maliciously and wilfully, with malice aforethought, maltreated Christopher Wright, from the effects of which he died on the 16th inst.'

A trial date was set for 31st March 1871.

The evidence given at the trial was compelling. Witnesses were all able to identify Ellis Parker and attest as to his actions on the night of 8th January and the early morning of 9th January. Dr Altham confirmed the extent of Christopher Wright's injuries, including a fractured skull, and stated that the injuries undoubtedly caused his death. Before retiring to consider their verdict, the jury were instructed by the judge that 'the old man had a right to lay hold of the prisoner, and had a right to use as much violence as he liked, even to the point of killing him, in putting him out of his house.' (not something which the law in the 21st century would permit a householder to do)

The jury returned a verdict of guilty of manslaughter. This may seem an extraordinarily lenient verdict by modern standards, considering the viciousness and unprovoked nature of the attack, and the frailness of the victim. However, along with extreme poverty, it is a comparatively common thread that permeates many murder trials of the period. Alcohol was frequently seen as a mitigating factor in crime; and not a contributory cause, with juries surprisingly unwilling to administer the death penalty.

Summing up, the judge spoke directly to the prisoner:

Ellis Parker, your conduct was as great an outrage as I have heard of for many years, and I cannot sufficiently express the

contempt I feel for the mode in which you behaved that night.
That you should answer his appeal to go; by using your immense
power on an old man and throwing him to the ground with all
your force, dragging him along the passage of his own house and
throwing him against a hard substance. If you had used a weapon
there would be not the least doubt that you would have been
found guilty absolutely of murder, and of murder for which there
could have been no forgiveness, and your life would have been
forfeited. Because you did not use a weapon the jury have thought
it right that you should not be charged with murder, but a more
gross and unmanly outrage I have seldom heard of. I consider it
my duty to sentence you to penal servitude for five years.

Ellis Parker served five years of hard labour and emerged
in 1876, a much weaker and subdued man. He died 10 years
later, in 1886, probably as a result of the harshness of his
chosen lifestyle.

The liquor licence of the Bay Horse Inn was revoked by
the local magistrate shortly after the death of Christopher
Wright and it became a shoe shop. The rear of the
shop was transformed into a 'selling out' shop, which
undoubtedly meant it continued to sell ale to locals. It
became known locally thereafter as The Pig and Whistle.

WHO KILLED MARY LEAROYD?
(PART ONE)

Ramsey MacDonald had just formed the first Labour
Government and Wilfred Rhodes, playing cricket for
Yorkshire, had taken his 4,000th first class wicket. There
were signs of an economic slowdown, queues at the Labour
Exchange were increasing. The Wall Street Crash and the
beginnings of the Great Depression were just eight weeks
away.

It was Saturday 24th August 1929 and another bustling
late summer's day in Ilkley. Mary Learoyd left her friend
Mrs Elliot's house, where she had been helping her cut
out a pattern for a dress. She departed Wilmot Road and
was next seen around 4.15pm, walking along The Grove
by her friend Mary Ellen Dance. Miss Dance asked Mary
if she would like to go to the Grove Picture House later
that evening to see a double bill, *Legions of the Condemned*,
followed by *The Modern Flapper*. Alfred Hitchcock had
just released *Blackmail*, Britain's first 'talkie', but the girls
could not see it as The Grove Picture House would not be
converted to sound until the following year. Mary Learoyd
would never realise her wish to see a 'talkie'.

Mary returned home to her parents' house in Sedbergh Park Road, a pleasant, if rather hilly, lane of recently built semi-detached villas. Although nearly 36 years of age, Mary was single and still lived at home. A slightly awkward girl, shy and ungainly, she had decided to remain at home and help nurse her mother and father, neither of whom were well. Her father helped at the  local church and Mary did too. She had several female friends, one of whom she was planning a holiday to Jersey with. Although she was not thought to have many male acquaintances, she was a member of the Ben Rhydding Operatic Society and was also known to regularly spend evenings at the home of the verger, Mr Elliot, playing parlour games and listening to music. Perhaps a little bit too friendly for the verger's wife's liking.

After eating with her parents Mary left the house in the steep and windy Sedbergh Park Road and headed into town. She was wearing a green dress, with a pale blue beret, a string of imitation ivory pearls and a matching flower in her buttonhole. She had on a light tweed coat to guard against the evening chill.

Between 7pm and 7.30pm Mary called into Mr Dobson's shop in Brook Street to buy a copy of the *Radio Times*. Mr Dobson would later recall that Mary's behaviour seemed odd, over excitable, and she was laughing. She was usually quiet and reserved. Around 8.30pm Mary's aunt, Maud

Rogers, spotted Mary crossing the road in the front of the library, heading towards the station. They exchanged a greeting but Mary did not tell her aunt where she was going. Almost immediately Miss Dance, the friend who had previously asked her to go to the cinema, was waiting in the queue outside the New Cinema and noticed Mary walking slowly along Brook Street, as if waiting for someone. The girls waved at each other and smiled.

Around 8.40pm she was seen in the queue outside the Grove Picture House by a young boy, although he could not be absolutely certain it was Mary. At 9pm Mary was witnessed by Fanny Fisher, apparently walking back in the direction of the library. There were no further confirmed sightings of Mary until 10.30pm, an hour and a half later, close to her home in Sedbergh Park Road. A lady named Alice Murray noticed Mary from her window. Mary was stood close to a telegraph pole talking to a man. He had his arm around her.

Ten minutes later another couple, Mr and Mrs Evans, were walking back up Sedbergh Park Road towards their home when they noticed a couple stood halfway between the houses which led through to an open area of waste land behind the buildings. This area, just off Cowpasture Road, was at the time a vacant building plot, mostly overgrown, sloping, and eventually leading to open moorland. Mrs Evans remembered the encounter distinctly.

As she drew nearer the couple, Mrs Evans was aware that the woman deliberately turned her back, as if trying to avoid being recognised. As Mr and Mrs Evans carried on walking along the road and past the couple, the woman made a conscious effort to simultaneously manoeuvre herself to avoid making eye contact. The man, too, seemed to be endeavouring not to be recognised. He was wearing a trilby hat, dark suit and carrying a raincoat under his arm. Even though Mrs Evans was unable to see the woman's face, she was almost certain it was Mary Learoyd. Firstly, the woman was slightly taller than the man (Mary Learoyd was 5' 8", above average height for a woman in Britain during the 1920s), and secondly because she recognised the light tweed coat the woman was wearing as being identical to the one she had often seen Mary in.

Just a few minutes later, at around 10.45pm, Mary Parchett was upstairs in her home in Sedbergh Park Road, about to retire for the night, when she was disturbed by the sound of a dog barking. Looking out of the window, she clearly saw in the moonlight a couple standing by her front gate. It was almost a full moon that night and the sky was cloudless. The couple were laughing and talking as they headed into the long grass on the waste land behind the houses. Mr Parchett called out of the window and told the couple to move on, but they ignored him and moved out of sight into the long grass. The Parchetts retired to bed and were not disturbed again.

Just a few moments later, a young man, John Skirrow, was walking his sweetheart Alice Kairs home from the cinema, along Cowpasture Road. As they passed the plot of waste land, they heard a scream and both instantly turned their heads to look across the road into the long grass opposite.

They distinctly saw a couple lying in the grass, bathed by the bright moonlight. Alice Kairs heard the woman say, in a phrase that would become the most infamous and haunting part of the investigation, 'If you wait, I will kiss you'. Assuming it was just a courting couple, John and Alice continued along the road. After John had walked Alice to her front door, he returned a few minutes later, back along Cowpasture Road. He could clearly make out the couple in the long grass but they did not make a sound as he passed them.

At the same time as the Parchetts and John Skirrow noticed the couple, Nellie Lister, a nursing sister at the Belle Vue nursing and maternity home, which overlooked Sedbergh Park and part of the vacant building plot, also overheard the couple as she looked out across the gardens towards the waste land. She was able to precisely describe what she heard:

I heard a man and a woman talking as they walked up the path. They sat on a seat at the top, not thirty yards from my window, and I could hear them talking plainly. I did not actually hear the conversation but I could hear a cultured woman's voice and the voice of an obviously well-educated Yorkshire man. I am positive that I would recognise that voice again. The couple sat on the seat for an hour, then walked away then came back. After some time the man became angry and excited.

Nellie Lister needed to return to a patient at 1.30am to administer an injection. Due to the exact timing required for the injection, she was able to be precise about the hour. As she closed the window she noticed that, 'the man was still agitated and his voice was raised in his excitement. The woman's voice was not raised.'

It would be the final sighting of Mary Learoyd alive.

Meanwhile, Mary's parents, at their home in Sedbergh Park Road, were surprised and a little worried when Mary did not return home. The roads were quiet now, and the public houses and cinemas were all shut. Perhaps, they thought to themselves, she had gone home to a friend's house and they would see her in the morning.

The following morning, Sunday 25th August 1929, Mrs Parchett had gone out into her garden, which bordered the waste land behind. As she looked beyond the iron railings at the boundary of her garden and into the bushes she noticed something strange. It was a lady's foot and the lower part of a leg sticking out from the undergrowth. She shouted to raise the alarm and her husband came out into the garden. The practically naked body was partially concealed by the long grass. It was that of Mary Learoyd, lying just 10 yards from the Parchett's garden and less than 100 yards from the safety of her own home.

Mr Parchett immediately contacted Ilkley Police Station and Inspector Marsh and Sergeant Baldwin hastened to the location. Realising the seriousness of the crime, extra officers from Otley and Wakefield were soon drafted in. Inspector Marsh carefully observed all the details from the crime scene. The actual murder appeared to have taken place underneath a nearby thorn tree, as the grass had been flattened and trampled, which suggested Mary had put up a vigorous struggle for her life. Her hat, shoes and other articles of clothing were found under the tree, but the body appeared to then have been dragged through the long grass and behind a thorny hedge. Her clothing had been removed, not carefully, but torn off in a frenzy. One of her silk stockings had been tied tightly around her neck, whilst the other had been used to tie her hands behind her back. Mary's face had been savagely beaten, to the extent that her nose, chin and jaw had been smashed. Her teeth had been driven in and her lips and face were heavily cut. It was thought that the injuries must have been caused by a heavy instrument rather than a fist, and this hypothesis seemed to be supported by the discovery of a large, bloodstained stone nearby. A post-mortem would be required to discover whether she had died of strangulation before being beaten.

Already dead, Mary had also been sexually assaulted in an horrific way, and her handbag then rifled. No money was found in her purse, which had been opened. As Mary had been planning a holiday to Jersey and no money was located at her home, it was assumed that the killer had made off with her savings – something in the region of £10-£15. Yet, strangely, her wristwatch had not been taken. The police were also puzzled that a greater effort had not been made to conceal the body. Had this been done, there was a good chance it may not have been uncovered for days.

While a crowd of morbid onlookers gathered at the gap in the hedge, hoping for a glimpse of the crime scene, the police began a thorough search of the open ground, scything and raking the ground in a frantic search for clues. Colonel Jacynth Coke, the Chief Constable of the West Riding, and Mr H Barraclough, the Assistant Chief Constable were both present to assist. By 6pm, two bloodhounds (Mystic and Mournful, who also feature in the chapter *The Cattle Mart Killer*) were drafted in to assist. However, after a few hours the scent was lost somewhere between the grounds of Ilkley Hall and Wells Road, and the dogs returned empty handed.

The police were perplexed from the outset by a series of puzzling questions. Had Mary gone willingly to this dark and secluded spot at night, or had she been attacked, rendered unconscious and dragged there? This seemed unlikely as the effort required to haul a woman of 5'8" across steep and rough ground would have been considerable. And there were no marks to indicate this. Yet, to all those who knew Mary, the thought that she would have ventured onto the vacant plot with a complete stranger, was unthinkable.

Who had she been waiting for on the previous evening when she had been seen by various witnesses in The Grove and Brook Street? Had she arranged to meet someone at the train station? If she had, then that person, assuming it was the same person who killed her would have missed the last train home. Why were there no sightings of her between 9pm and 10.30pm? The library had already closed by that hour. The most likely explanation is that she had visited the cinema, as the film times corresponded, however, no-one could be found who could remember seeing her there.

Was Mary with someone she knew well, so felt comfortable in walking onto the vacant plot of land? This seemed the most likely explanation, as several witnesses had seen her arm-in-arm and talking to a man. Yet her parents were adamant that she had no male friends.

Wild rumours began to circulate in the town. Conceivably she had been with a married man. A good deal of soul-searching was undertaken as many in the town did not want to examine too closely the morals of Ilkley's young men and women.

Perhaps, not wanting to believe that Mary would have gone willingly on the waste land that night, speculation grew that she had been drugged by a hypodermic syringe. It was claimed that marks found on her arm were evidence of this. However, Dr Sutherland, the pathologist, stated that this method would have been very unlikely due to the amount of time required for the drug to take effect, and the difficulty of injecting a person if they were struggling. Dr Sutherland also reported that, if an anaesthetic such as chloroform had been used, he would have been unable to detect it. At the post-mortem Dr Sutherland also confirmed that the cause of death was the trauma caused by the injuries to Mary's face and that the silk stocking was probably applied when she was just dying or was already dead. Some of her other injuries and the sexual assault had been inflicted after death. There was no trace of poison in Mary's body.

A young man, who knew Mary, claimed that she had been molested a few months earlier; and that she had asked him to escort her home on several occasions. However, this story was unsubstantiated by Mary's parents or any of her friends.

Meanwhile, the police continued their painstaking search of local woods, moorland, and outbuildings. Garages and cars were checked, house to house enquires were undertaken and a reward was offered.

WEST RIDING OF YORKSHIRE
£100 REWARD

Whereas Mary Learoyd was murdered
at Ilkley on the 24th August last,
£100 reward is offered to any person
who will give information
leading to the arrest and conviction of the murder

J d'E COKE, Colonel Chief Constable
of the West Riding of Yorkshire County Police Headquarters
Wakefield, 4th Sept, 1929

The £100 reward, which was never claimed, is today's equivalent of approximately £6,300.

Unfortunately, the police were pulled in several directions across the country as they chased lead after lead. Some were promising, while others were speculative and bizarre.

On the day following the murder, detectives raced to Baildon in motor cars after receiving reports of a stranger hiding in Hawksworth Wood and foaming at the mouth. However, no such person was ever found.

About 7.30am on the Sunday morning, three hours before Mary's body was discovered, a young man hailed a passing motorist on the road between Skipton and Addingham and asked for a lift. The motorist said he travelling to Preston and the young man seemed happy to be taken there. He was described as about 25 years of age, 5'7" in height, with a fresh complexion and a gold tooth on the right side. He was dressed in a blue serge suit and had several scratches on his face.

A taxi driver in Ilkley picked up a man at 10.45pm on the night of the murder, only 150 yards from the scene. The man seemed excitable and said, 'Drive me to Addingham'. The man then changed his mind and requested that he be driven to Skipton, where he jumped out, throwing the taxi driver a crumpled 10-shilling note. Police examined the note but could not find any forensic evidence on it. Once the timeline of Mary's last movements were known, the excitable man jumping in the taxi cab was ruled out.

A man in Selby, who seemed to express a deep interest in the crime, was reported to the police who rushed to question him. However, he was soon released. In another incident, a child spotted the face of a man at the window of a house that was thought to be deserted. This was investigated, but the man had already vanished. Several witnesses also recalled seeing a man with a limp and uneven shoulders.

In the weeks leading up to Mary's murder, there were various reports of a man exposing himself and yelling obscenities near the local Cow and Calf rock crag. Three weeks prior to the murder, a labourer, John Tordoff, witnessed the same man follow a woman up Cowpasture Road and grab her by the arm. He was described as thin, sallow and slightly bow legged.

Within a week or so, the search for Mary's killer seemed to grind to a halt. All the promising leads had effectively dried up. The public clamoured for answers and, no doubt, the investigating officers were under pressure from their superiors. However, the investigation was about to take a surprising turn.

WHO KILLED MARY LEAROYD?
(PART TWO)

The next stage in the hunt for the killer of Mary Learoyd
may seem far-fetched to a 21st century audience. However,
it was not considered so in 1929. Interest in spiritualism
and bridging the gap between this world and the next
had gathered momentum following the Great War. The
practice had many high profile and influential supporters,
such as Sir Arthur Conan Doyle and Cora Scott. Many
grieving relatives, in a desperate attempt to make sense
of their tragic loss, sought the help of mediums. With
so many soldiers' bodies never recovered, the comfort
that could be taken by an encounter with the spirit of
a deceased relative was perhaps more understandable
then than it appears today. There were, of course, many
charlatans purporting to be in contact with the dead, and
only too willing to take payment from grieving families for
their services.

Local clairvoyant, the Rev Tweedale, grandly entered the
local police station offering his assistance. Mrs Newton,
a local fortune teller, also claimed to have twice spoken
to Mary. The police, perhaps increasing in desperation,

even assisted a Liverpool spiritualist, Bertram Scarff, by allowing Mary Learoyd's beret to be driven to his home in order to assist his attempts at communication with her spirit. After some histrionics and pantomime, in which he claimed to be possessed by the spirit of Mary and then of a well-educated observer, the police were still no closer to catching their killer.

However, perhaps the most intriguing séance of all took place in Bradford on the 17th September. A local clairvoyant claimed to have been contacted by the spirit of Mary, who told him, 'of a man who went into a field and asked which was the best field for mushrooms'. This seemingly bizarre and meaningless sentence, however, reminded a Ben Rhydding man of an incident which had taken place in the early morning after the murder, which he had not previously connected with the crime. The man explained that:

I had been gathering mushrooms in the meadow, when a man came up to me and asked, "Is this the best field for mushrooms?". I laughed at the way he put the question. He walked very fast up and down the field. I noticed particularly that the man was wearing white shirt cuffs and that he had to jerk his wrists several times to keep them up. He had no bag for gathering mushrooms. He was dressed in a blue serge suit and light fawn coat. His right hand was wrapped with some sort of bandage, and there was a blood mark, I think on his cuff. He told me he had hurt his hand in getting through the hedge.

The man was never traced.

Rumours continued to circulate in Ilkley. Gossip spread around the town that the guilty man had drowned himself by jumping in the River Wharfe. Police were unable to find a body and no one was reported missing. Meanwhile, Mary's brother, Eric Learoyd, received a mysterious telegram, delivered to his home in Colbert Avenue which bore just five words – 'Be a man and tell'. Eric Learoyd immediately handed the telegram to the police and made a statement to the newspapers:

I have given them all the details I can think of concerning my sister that could be of any possible assistance. I have had previous letters of this kind, but there have been rumours that I was in some way connected with the crime itself. I understand that these rumours were mainly circulated in the Bradford district. There is absolutely no truth in them whatever, and I denied them point blank as soon I heard of them.

Under increasing pressure the police did not rely solely on leads from the public, but pursued their own lines of enquiry.

Officers spent some time investigating Mary's background. Despite the image of Mary as a spinster, with no male friends and dedicated to the church, a different picture emerged. Dorothy Earnshaw, who was well acquainted with Mary, reported seeing her on the previous Sunday to the murder in Burley Woodhead. Again, she appeared to be waiting for someone and, again, she seemed to turn her head and linger in a gateway as if wishing to avoid being seen.

Doris Baker informed police that she had seen Mary with a strange man, about a year prior to the murder, walking down Cowpasture Road from the direction of the Moors. Doris remembered teasing Mary about the incident, but never found out the man's identity. She did remember his appearance, however. Aged about 30, clean shaven, smartly dressed, with dark hair.

The stories about Mary's relationship with Mr Elliot, the verger, came under scrutiny too.

Mary's brother, Eric, was questioned by the police about the relationship, saying, 'One or two of us rather resented the intimacy with the Elliots. She was at Church at lot with Elliot alone. Several times they had sent across to Kemp's Café for tea and they had it together in the vestry. I thought she was too free with a married man.' Mr Elliot was also interviewed, and it seems that his behaviour, as a married man, and a verger, in the 1920s, must surely have raised some eyebrows locally. He told the police:

She asked me to go to her house during the same week, mentioning Saturday night, she told me that her father and mother were going to be out and that she would be alone. I arrived about 8.30pm and left about 10. Miss Learoyd gave me a light supper, tea and biscuits, etc. No intoxicants were consumed. We spent the time listening to the wireless and talking.

The police were interested enough in Mr Elliot's movements to thoroughly check his alibi for the night of 24th August. He too had been out in Ilkley and was seen by various witnesses before arriving home around 10.40pm.

His wife was not in; but arrived home shortly afterwards.
Did he go out again, after his wife had fallen asleep? The
sequence certainly matches the times that Mary was seen
by witnesses from 10.45pm onwards. However, Mr Elliot
was certainly not with Mary earlier in the evening as his
movements up until 10.40pm were well documented by the
police.

Had Mary been secretly meeting two different men? Her
apparent tryst in Burley Woodhead the previous week, and
also with someone else? Had one man spotted the other,
then followed them in a fit of jealousy. Perhaps killing
Mary after her first lover had left? The attack on Mary
certainly had an agenda of violence and anger, perhaps
even of humiliation, far beyond that of mere lust.

If she did have a secret lover, who had left her there alone,
he certainly never came forward. Was he a married man,
or too scared that he would become a suspect? These were
all questions that puzzled detectives during the frustrating
investigation.

Perhaps the strongest suspect known to the police was
a 24-year-old engineer from Bradford, called Samuel
Henry Exley. An arrogant young man, Sam Exley had
already earned a reputation in Bradford for drunkenness,
obscene language and for forcing his attentions on women.
Bradford Police had already received several complaints
from young ladies in Bradford regarding his inappropriate
approaches to them. Exactly two weeks prior to the murder
of Mary Learoyd, on 10th August, Exley had appeared
in Bradford City Police Court on three charges of using

abusive and threatening language towards three young woman who did not yield to his demands. He was fined 10 shillings, plus costs. He was then charged with the violent assault and attempted rape of a young nurse; however, the case was adjourned; as the victim was unable to identify her attacker in court.

Exley was released on bail. However, one of the female jurors at the trial, Elizabeth Collins the manageress of the Royal Oak in Ilkley, remembered him. She had seen Exley, around 9.15pm, at a dance in Ilkley on the night of Mary's murder. Many other witnesses had also noticed Exley, including Herbert Horseman, to whom Exley had remarked, 'I'm off, I have a tart to meet.' It seemed that Bradford was becoming too uncomfortable for Exley and he had chosen Ilkley as his new playground.

Police were keen to interview Exley and arrived at his lodging in Granville Road, Frizinghall in Bradford, at 11.30pm on the day of discovery of Mary's body. Interestingly, his landlady confirmed to the police that Exley had not returned home until 2.15am that morning, then stayed in bed until lunchtime. There, hanging in his room, was a blue suit matching the suit described by witnesses who had previously seen Mary walking with a man.

Exley was questioned by police and provided an elaborate tale explaining that he had met a man with a one leg, and together they had spent the evening chatting to girls at the Wheatsheaf Hotel and the Royal in Ilkley. After that, he claimed, the girl had suggested to him that he buy her a box of chocolates. Exley then asked her, 'what if I do?', to which the girl replied, 'We'll go onto the moors and have a bit of love.' However, Exley claimed the girl had given him the slip when he had gone to the gents wc at the Kings Hall and he had ended up walking through Ben Rhydding, eventually catching the last bus as far as Burley.

The two girls the men had been flirting with were both located and confirmed the story regarding the early part of the evening. Many parts of Exley's story matched details given by witnesses, the blue suit, a man with a limp, the fact that he was in Ilkley. However, his timeline during that evening could not be made to fit the circumstances around Mary's death. Without modern forensics his blue suit was given a cursory inspection only, 'held under a strong electric light, it showed no signs of roughage'. Would a more detailed examination have revealed telling evidence? We will never know. Could Exley have returned to Sedbergh Park Road after catching the bus to Burley in Wharfedale - if, indeed, he was ever on that bus? Assuming that he had got off the bus at Burley, he feasibly could have walked back to Ilkley, a journey of about 4 miles, in an hour or so, placing him in Cowpasture Road around 12.30am. However, there were no sightings of Exley back in Ilkley, or journeying towards the town, that night. Coupled with the fact that his landlady was certain that he had returned to Bradford by 2.15am - a journey he could not have accomplished on foot, within that time frame.

There are, however, several possibilities which make Exley the prime suspect in the murder of Mary Learoyd. He had a low regard for women and authority, seeing himself as superior and of a higher intelligence. His sexual offences, and we possibly only have knowledge of a small number of them, already seemed to be escalating by 1928/9. Did he meet and walk with Mary Leoroyd? It certainly was typical of his behaviour, and his description matched that of the man seen early the following morning, and with Mary late on the Saturday night - blue suit, dark hair, appearing to be well spoken with a Yorkshire accent and slightly shorter than her. Exley certainly had the bravado to undertake such an attack, but would he really have progressed from being charged with attempted rape to a cold blooded murder, with such a precise modus operandi?

Perhaps the answer lies in what Sam Exley did after he was questioned and released by the police for the murder of Mary Learoyd. Just a few weeks after Mary's death (while still on bail for the previous attempted rape). Exley was charged with 'assault with intent to commit a grave offence' against a 21-year-old typist. He pleaded not guilty. Exley, on the exterior, appeared charming. He took the young lady for supper at the County Restaurant. When she wished to catch the bus home to Cutler Heights, Exley offered to hail a taxi, and climbed in with her. He then attempted to assault her in the taxi, but she resisted. Exley ordered the driver to 'run around for a bit'. He then shut the window between the driver and the passenger seats and punched the girl three times in the face. She screamed, after which he forced his fingers into her mouth, causing it to bleed. At this point, the taxi driver hurriedly pulled up alongside a policeman, and Exley was arrested. When the policeman opened the door of the taxi the girl was lying across the floor, between the seats, with her clothing disarranged. He had squeezed her throat so tightly that the string of beads she was wearing were indented into her neck. She later testified against Exley in court, 'He was like a madman. He squeezed my throat and afterwards I discovered bruises on my neck. I felt as though I were being choked.'

Exley was tried at the West Riding Assizes, just 10 weeks after Mary Learoyd's murder, for this attack, and the previous charge for which he had been on bail at the time. For the original offence, the witnesses explained that Exley had met a girl when leaving the Branch Hotel in Shipley in August. He asked the girl if he could walk her home. In the half light, she thought it was someone she knew, however, when she realised it wasn't she hurried on ahead. Exley caught her up and put his arm around her waist. He tried to kiss her. She struggled and cried out, 'Let go! I want to go home'. For a moment she broke free; but Exley grabbed her and pulled her into a dark passageway between the houses. He attempted to kiss her again. When she refused, he dragged her into some bushes behind the buildings. She screamed for help and Exley coldly told her, 'If you make that noise again, I will clout you in the face.' He then hit her and attempted to assault her, his hand so firmly over her mouth she felt as if she were choking. Fortunately for the girl, her screams were overheard and the sound of footsteps approaching prevented Exley from going any further. The girl managed to struggle free, and escape. As she ran away Exley yelled out, 'I'm not finished with you yet'.

He then returned towards the Branch Hotel, where he was later arrested. On being charged he replied, 'This is ridiculous. I had no idea she was a respectable girl.'

His obvious contempt for authority was shown during his sentencing. Exley was found guilty of two attempts of assault and attempted rape and sentenced to five years' hard labour. Mr Justice Hawke told Exley, 'It is quite evident that your moral code is of the lowest possible order. It cannot be tolerated for a moment that respectable women should be treated in this way. Do you have anything to say?' Exley smiled, winked, and replied, 'I don't think so'.

He was taken to Wakefield Jail where he served four years of his five-year sentence. During his four years in prison there were no similar sexual assaults or attacks in the Ilkley or Shipley areas. It is almost certain that an attack of the kind suffered by Mary Learoyd would have been accompanied by other offences.

Exley was released from Wakefield Prison in August 1933. He married shortly afterwards and moved to Northampton into a house already owned by his wife. In November 1934 he opened a fish and chip shop in Kingsthorpe Road, Northampton, financed by some money left to him by his mother.

Early in 1935 he met a young lady, named Elizabeth Mack, who worked in a Northampton laundry. Exley accosted her in Gold Street, put his arm around her, and asked her to accompany him across the racecourse, however, the couple ended up in his room above the fish and chip shop (presumably his wife was away). Between the hours of 10.15pm on Saturday 9th February 1935 and the early hours of Sunday morning, he sexually assaulted her and subjected her to a violent attack. Elizabeth was found wandering in a daze at Kingsthorpe Hollow and Exley was arrested shortly afterwards. At his trial details emerged that bore a shocking similarity to the murder of Mary Learoyd. Police discovered evidence of a struggle at Exley's home, showing that Elizabeth had attempted to fight him off. She had suffered from lacerations to her scalp and face, a broken jaw, bruising to the throat and to the chest.

In court Elizabeth Mack explained that Exley offered her, '10 shillings if you let me hit you.'

She replied, 'If you must hit me, hit me on the arm. He then clutched at my throat. I can remember catching hold of his fingers, and saying "don't, don't", and I remember no more until I regained consciousness.'

Elizabeth regained consciousness surrounded by broken glass. She had been hit over the head with a heavy milk bottle and left for dead. She explained to the court that she had felt, 'like a cornered rat.'

Exley initially pleaded not guilty to three charges, including one of attempted murder, but eventually changed to his plea to 'guilty of unlawful wounding'. He was sentenced to seven years' imprisonment by Justice Hilbery, who described him as 'a dangerous and vile monster'.

Following his release from prison in 1942, his wife divorced him. Exley died in 1953 at the age of 48, taking details of any other crimes he may have committed to the grave with him.

But for Exley's landlady confirming that he returned home at 2.15am on the night of Mary Learoyd's murder, the case for Exley being her murderer appears to be a strong one. Did he bribe, persuade or threaten her into lying on his behalf, thus throwing the police off the scent? If we accept that as a hypothesis, then everything else falls into place.

Even if we assume that Exley's landlady was telling the truth, and he was home by 2.15am as he claimed, it appears to leave us with an even more unlikely proposition. If Exley was not the killer of Mary Learoyd that must mean, by default, that two serial rapists, with the same modus operandi, were present in Ilkley at the same time on the same evening. Statistically speaking, that seems almost an impossibility.

Returning to 1929, and the events that followed the murder of Mary Learoyd, her funeral was held at Ilkley Parish Church, and she was interred at Ilkley Cemetery. Sadly, although large crowds lined the route of the funeral procession, her parents were unable to attend, due to ill health. The tragic news of Mary's death had severely worsened their already failing constitutions. From his sick bed, Mary's father wrote to the press, 'Thank you for all the sympathy and help in thought, word, and deed given to myself and my family. It has helped materially to lighten our burden and my heart is too full to say more than thank you.'

Despite their huge efforts, the police investigation ultimately fizzled out. 1,300 interviews were held, thousands of man hours were racked up, and 453 statements were taken. Yet, the burden of limited forensics, too many red herrings and wild goose chases, which sent officers flitting across the country, wasted the time and resources available. Their tenacious efforts to investigate Sam Exley were ultimately thwarted by the evidence of one witness. Had they possessed the benefit of hindsight, as we do now, and known more of Exley's other crimes, perhaps they could have unpicked his story to a greater degree. We will never know.

In 1931, a Commissioner's Report was sent to Scotland Yard lamenting the failure of various police forces across the country to clear up an ever-increasing number of unsolved murders. The Mary Learoyd case was one of those included in the report.

Public dissatisfaction with the investigation in Ilkley was palpable for many years, as was anxiety that the unknown killer might strike again. This was aptly demonstrated in October 1934 when Emily Yeoman was murdered in an almost identical fashion in Middleton Woods, in Leeds. The *Daily Mirror* carried the following headline:

> ### *STRANGLED GIRL: SENSATIONAL THEORY ILKLEY CRIME RECALLED*
>
> *The Same Brute at Large – Both Women Strangled*

Ultimately, an acquaintance of Emily's, David Blake, despite strongly protesting his innocence, was found guilty on the thinnest possible evidence, notwithstanding the fact that an unknown man was spotted leaving Middleton Woods in the early hours of the morning, and never identified.

Interestingly, the murder was committed just six weeks after Sam Exley's release from Wakefield Prison. Sam Exley moved to Northampton three weeks after Emily Yeoman's murder and was never questioned in relation to her death.

DEATH AT RICHMOND STABLES

During the Victorian era Richmond in North Yorkshire was a genteel place, attracting wealthy landowners, race enthusiasts and stable owners. The town had managed to escape the worst ravages of Victorian crime and sensational newspaper headlines until two weeks before Christmas 1865, when the following sensational story was emblazoned across the *Yorkshire Post* and many of the country's newspapers:

'SHOCKING MURDER BY A JOCKEY
AT RICHMOND, YORKSHIRE.
It if not often that the usually quiet town of Richmond is
disturbed by the committal of the crime which we have to
record, and the announcement of a murder having taken
place in the town is made still more painful by the fact
that the perpetrator of it is a youth who hitherto had borne
comparatively good character.'

Britain was very much a country of two halves
in 1865. The poorer classes worked long hours
for little reward, often enduring dreadful living
conditions, or the workhouse if they fell foul of their
landlord or employer. It was hoped that the recent
passing of the *Poor Law Act* in Westminster would
improve conditions in the most austere institutions.
Meanwhile, the rich enjoyed new luxuries and
leisure pass-times. Holidays, reading, art, and horse
racing – the sport of kings. One such man was Mr
James Watson, a wealthy trainer and stable owner,
who owned Richmond's most prestigious stables and
training yard, named Belleisle, located just outside
the town and close to the River Swale. Richmond
Racecourse was celebrating its 100th anniversary in
1865 and Thursday 14th December had been a busy
and eventful day at Belleisle Stables. Daylight was now
fast disappearing and the staff were occupied, either
in the large saddle-room, tidying the tackroom, or
preparing to close the stables for the night.

Meanwhile, raised voices emanated from the
passageway which connected the main stable to
the saddle-room. Robert Roberts, James Watson's
head groom and manager at the yard, stood in the
passageway with one of the young jockeys, sixteen-
year-old Francis Lawrence. The unmistakable sound
of a fracas between the two men could be clearly
heard by those in the saddle-room. Angry voices,
followed by the sound of a tussle, a sickening thud,
and the sound of a lantern crashing to the stone

floor. After a brief moment of silence, came the sound of footsteps leaving the stable by the far door. Rushing into the passageway, the staff found the body of Robert Roberts lying prostrate on the floor, by the stable entrance, with a pitchfork protruding from his head. The pitchfork had entered Robert's skull with such force, that one prong had entered his mouth, passing out through the back of his cranium, the middle prong had pierced his right eye socket embedding itself in his skull. The third prong had narrowly missed Roberts' left eyesocket. Blood was still gushing from the wounds. Young Francis Lawrence, the jockey, was nowhere to be seen.

Miraculously, Roberts appeared to be clinging onto life and medical assistance was urgently sent for. In an effort to relieve his suffering, one of the staff attempted to pull the pitchfork out of Robert's head. However, the implement had been thrust into his skull with such intensity, it would require two men to remove it. The doctor from Richmond arrived but, alas, it was too late, and Robert Roberts succumbed to his terrible injuries shortly after the attack.

The police were summoned and Francis Lawrence was soon located, cowering in the hayloft above the main stable. He was in a state of shock and claimed the whole incident had been an awful accident. A young jockey of the utmost promise, Mr James Watson had taken Lawrence under his wing. Although only sixteen, Lawrence had already ridden at all the major race meetings in the north of England; Newcastle, Carlisle, Catterick and Richmond.

The young man was arrested and a coroner's inquest was ordered to determine exactly what had taken place; and to ascertain if Lawrence should face trial for murder. Oddly, local opinion seemed to radiate a noticeable feeling of sympathy for Francis Lawrence, who was described as likeable, hard-working and pleasant. Little mention of the victim was made.

With no witnesses to the incident itself, and the young jockey's previous good conduct it was decided that a charge of manslaughter, and not murder, should be brought against him. A trial date was set for Tuesday 27th March 1866, at the Assizes in York. The case created a great deal of public interest and excitement, as a huge crowd gathered, all hoping to witness the proceedings from the public gallery. Throughout the trial the courtroom remained packed, with many more waiting in the street outside. Mr Justice Keating oversaw the proceedings, while Mr Skidmore Q.C. appearing for the Crown and Mr Shepherd Q.C. for the defence.

The prosecution opened their case with Mr Skidmore stating,

'The facts of the case are of a very painful nature. The prosecution alleges that the prisoner caused the death of the

deceased, and yet, though nobody saw the offence committed, the evidence would be of such a nature as to require the attention of the jury. At the time of his death, Robert Roberts had the superintendence and management of the lads in the stables. He had also to lock up the stables at night. On the evening in question about a quarter past eight o'clock the deceased went into the saddle-room of the establishment of Mr. Watson, and requested that Francis Lawrence and another boy fill a boiler for the use of the horses the following morning. The prisoner refused to do so; saying that he was attending to a horse, and alleging that it was not his duty to look to the filling of the boiler, and that it should be done by a younger lad. The deceased man, Roberts, left the place for a short time, and returned to the saddle-room five minutes later. Then he saw the prisoner again and remonstrated with him. *What then transpired will be made clear in the evidence. It will be shown by the defence that the deceased hit the prisoner with a large key, and that Lawrence then rushed out of the place and Roberts followed him.'*

The prosecution then alleged that Lawrence had hurled a stable fork at Roberts, *'which struck him on the head, thereby causing his death'*. When Lawrence was challenged with this offence he indicated that Roberts had struck him first, on the head with a large, heavy key.

Next to give evidence was the police constable who had arrested Lawrence. He testified that, *'I taxed the boy with the offence. When I did so the prisoner told me he had "jobbed the fork, but not intended it to injure the man".'*

(Jobbing is an archaic expression meaning to prod or thrust a pointed instrument in someone's direction, usually as a threat).

The prosecution then called **Ralph Davison**, a farmer also employed by Mr Watson, who testified:

'I recollect the 14ᵗʰ December, I was in the saddle-room, that was about eight o'clock. Lawrence was then present, and Roberts came in and told him to fill the boiler. To this the boy objected because it was not his business. Mr Roberts then left the room. Roberts then went out, but I saw him come back in again a few minutes later. I then found the deceased some short time afterwards in the passage leading from the saddle-room. *The saddle-room is a large place, and is approached through a large passage. Opposite the door is a fork-rack. The passage is about four feet wide. On this occasion I saw nothing from the time Roberts saw me, till I heard his lantern fall when I went to him'.*

Mr Davison was then asked if he knew why, if Lawrence had claimed the incident was accidental, he had chosen to hide in the hayloft? *'I was not present when the prisoner was taken into custody,'* Davison replied, *'but the hayloft is near the saddle-room and the boys are in the habit of going into there. There is nothing unusual in it'.*

The next witness, the groom Edward Messenger, stated:

'On the day in question, I was in the saddle-room of the establishment, and saw the prisoner and Mr Roberts. Mr

Roberts came into the saddle-room and ordered the prisoner and another boy to fill a boiler, but both objected. Roberts then left the saddle-room, and was absent for a quarter of an hour. When he returned, be hit the prisoner on the back of the head with his open fist, On this happening, the prisoner, Francis Lawrence, went in a stooping position, in the passage, and Mr Roberts followed him. Quickly after this, Davison, one of the stable men, called my attention to the passage, and there I found that Roberts was wounded by a hayfork in his face, and that Davison was supporting him. We pulled the fork out of Roberts' face. I did not at that time see the prisoner, as the place was dark. The forks hang in a rack in the passage'.

Edward Messenger's evidence seemed to contradict the prosecution's case, in that he claims to have seen some of the incident take place, and he also mentions the presence of another boy (Hugh Harrison). This inconsistency does not appear to have been seized upon by either side, nor by Mr Justice Keating. Instead, the cross-examination of the witnesses seems to have been chiefly concerned with the alleged presence of a key in the hand of Robert Roberts at the moment he struck Francis Lawrence:-

'Mr Messenger, when the deceased struck the prisoner, did he have a key in his hand?'

I cannot swear to it, Sir, and, when the prisoner ran out of the room, I cannot swear that Roberts ran after him, or that he struck the boy rapidly'.

The next witness, stable boy Hugh Harrison, seems to cast doubt on both the prosecution and defence cases:

'I was on that day in the saddle-room. I heard Mr Roberts order me and Lawrence to fill the boiler, and Lawrence said "All right". Lawrence left the room, and returned in five or ten minutes. Roberts also left, and returned quickly, and without saying anything he struck Lawrence on the head with his hand. I saw that Roberts had a lamp in his other hand, but I did not observe that he had anything else in it. Roberts never spoke before he hit Lawrence on the head. I cannot tell whether Roberts had a key in his hand when he struck Lawrence.'

Hugh Harrison's evidence also seems to cast doubt on whether Mr Roberts was actually holding a key in his hand at the time, which certainly did not assist the case for the defence. Nevertheless, Harrison's recollection that Francis Lawrence had agreed to light the boiler, seems at odds with the other witnesses' version of events.

Harrison continued, *'I was present when the prisoner was taken into custody from the hayloft, and I heard Lawrence say that he "picked up the fork without intending to injure him".'*

Police Constable Thomas Fawcett from Richmond Police was called next to try and shed some light on the puzzling affair:

'In consequence of information I received, I went to Belleisle Stables on the 14th December, a little after nine o'clock in

the evening. There I went into the saddle-room, and saw Roberts. I assisted in carrying him into the washhouse. He was then quite dead. I next went in search of the prisoner, and I found him in the hayloft. I said not a word to him before he spoke, and then he said, "The man has struck me over the head with a key." I told him that Roberts was dead, and he was charged with killing him. Lawrence said, "He struck me over the head with a key, and I jobbed the fork, not intending to injure him." The prisoner was crying when I took him in.'

Dr John Bowes from Richmond then gave the customary medical evidence,

'I was called to Belleisle on the night in question. I got there just before Roberts died. He was then scarcely conscious, and died soon afterwards. I found a wound at his right eye. I remained with him till his death. I made a post-mortem examination, and I found that a prong of the fork had penetrated the head and brain of the deceased an inch and a half, and this was the cause of death. There must have been considerable force used to get the fork into the deceased's head.'

Mr Shepherd, cross-examining for the defence, enquired, *'Doctor Bowes, is it possible that if a fork fell, or was knocked, from the rack it might accidentally cause death?'*

The Doctor replied, *'I suppose that if a fork were to fall from the rack, and a man fell upon it, that might cause death'.*

'Thank you, Doctor. No further questions.'

Next came the case for the defence who, from the outset, played their only card – that of Francis Lawrence's previous good character. The impressive figure of the stable owner Mr Watson was asked to testify to Lawrence's character,

'Lawrence,' he attested, *'has been at Belleisle for six years, coming to us as an orphan. He bears, and has always borne, a very good character. His age, I think, is 16 years. I have known the boy all the time he has been there. He has always borne a particularly good character. Lawrence had also hitherto borne an irreproachable character for quietness, good behaviour, and good temper. He was a boy of good and peaceful habits.'*

The final witness for the defence was a crucial, if somewhat surprising one. The Chief Constable of Gateshead Police, John Elliot, was presented to the court. Mr Elliot had found Francis Lawrence in 1858 as a young boy, deprived of parents, hungry and homeless. The Chief Constable had placed the boy in the 'Shoeblack Brigade', (an early police initiative to provide employment for orphans on the streets of Gateshead). Mr Elliot stated *'I did from time-to-time exercise parental care and authority for the prisoner. He was always a fine, well-behaved boy. I afterwards found him an apprenticeship with Mr. James Watson.'*

Mr Shepherd summed up the case for the defence by addressing the jury directly,

'Members of the jury, you have heard the testimony of these fine men. Surely, therefore, the prisoner was not likely to be guilty of such a crime as the one imputed to him and was not likely to have committed such an act as the one with which he was charged. My learned counsel for the prosecution could not attempt to justify the act if it were done, but there really did not appear, from the evidence, to have been any crime committed. The whole case was an accident. I stand here in the name of the poor orphan to tell you, the jury, that he never did cause the death of Roberts, and I challenge you to say if you could decide otherwise. The boy had done his duty in the stable. He had attended to the horses, and he did nothing to excite the anger of Roberts. Roberts, however, became angry. He then went up to the boy and struck him on the head with a key, and then the lad, in trying to evade more punishment, ran out of the room in a stooping position and Roberts after him. Then Roberts was afterwards found to have been killed by a fork, and it is for you, the jury, alone to say how that stab was occasioned.'

Mr Justice Keating sought clarification on one point, regarding exactly how the forks had been secured on the wall, and *'if a person hastily going into the passage might knock down a fork, and thence fall against it'*.

It took the jury only minutes to return a verdict of *'Not guilty'*, which was received with loud applause in the gallery. On the steps outside the court Francis Lawrence received an ovation from the crowd.

And so, this remarkable case concluded. A case riddled with contradictions. Although Lawrence had admitted to 'jobbing' the pitchfork at Mr Roberts, rather than the, frankly implausible, explanation that Roberts had knocked the pitchfork from its rack resulting in the implement somehow embedding itself deep into his skull, does not seem to have been properly examined. When coupled with the force with which the weapon had embedded itself into the victim, this important point appears to have been completely overlooked by the prosecution. It seems that the glowing character references from the Chief Constable of Gateshead and the wealthy trainer Mr Watson, taken together with the less than sympathetic demeanour of the victim, carried far more weight with the jury than any inconsistences with the various versions of events.

The body of Robert Roberts was returned to his wife and children in Hull for burial. Francis Lawrence stayed on as a jockey for Mr Watson, continuing to have a degree of success on the racetrack. He appears to have remained trouble free for the rest of his life, perhaps justifying the faith shown in him.

It seems, that in an era where forensic evidence was simply not available, good character may well have been the best defence.

ACKNOWLEDGEMENTS

Kevin and Jayne Ramage, The Grove Bookshop, Ilkley,
The Watermill Bookshop, Aberfeldy, Lesley Christian,
Ellen McBride, Dales Community Archive, High Royds
Hospital Archives, St Michael's Church at Linton in Craven,
National Archives Kew, Find My Past, Family Search,
Settle Graveyard Project, The Bank of England, England
GenWeb Project, Visit Yorkshire, Yorkshire Family
Research.

BIBLIOGRAPHY

The Yorkshire Post, Bradford Daily Telegraph, Bradford
Observer, Leeds Times, Dundee Courier, Liverpool Echo,
The Times, The Daily Telegraph, The Observer, Ilkley
Gazette, British Newspaper Archive, Leeds Museum,
True Crime Enthusiast, Barnsley Chronicle, Nottingham
Journal, Shipley Times & Express, Harrogate Herald,
Shipley Times, Capital Punishment UK Database,
Lancaster Gazette, Todmorden Advertiser, Hebden Bridge
Newsletter, Yorkshire Murder, by Stephen Wade, Haunted
Histories, The Hound of the Baskervilles, by Sir Arthur
Conan Doyle, Haunted Hostelries, Armley Jail Archives,
Tales From The Dales, Northern Life Magazine, On Ilkley
Moor by Tim Binding, Brimham Rocks by Ebenezer Elliot,
The Haunted Homes and Family Traditions of Great
Britain by John Ingram, The History of the Timbles and
Snowden by William Grainge, Belfast Times, Broadmoor
Hospital Archives, UK Court Database, The History of Her
Majesty's Inspectorate of Constabulary by Richard Cowley
and Peter Todd, Richmond & Ripon Chronicle, Hampshire
Advertiser, Northamptonshire Courier, Nottinghamshire
Journal, Evening Sentinel, Sheffield Daily Telegraph,

Daily Herald, Daily Mirror, Leeds Mercury, The Shields Daily News, The Yorkshire Observer, Evening News, The Leader, Northern Whig, The Railway Navvies by Terry Cole, Life and Tradition in the Yorkshire Dales by Marie Hartley and Joan Ingilby, Life in Victorian Britain by Michael Paterson, Victorian Law by Alan Evans, Violence, Manliness and Criminal Justice in Victorian England by Martin J Wiener, Testimony and Advocacy in Victorian Law, Literature, and Theology by Jan-Melissa Schramm, Strong Representations: Narrative and Circumstantial Evidence in England by Alexander Welsh, The Totnes and Devon Times, Halifax Daily Courier, Wikipedia.

If you enjoyed The Dark Side of the Dales, you might be interested in the author's research into the notorious 1766 murder of Dr Petty in the bustling Dales market town of Grassington.

Through detailed research, including the uncovering of some documentation, eyewitness statements and newspaper reports from the time, Mark has compared and contrasted a well-known Victorian version of the story, with the known facts, and asked the question – Fact or Fiction? Who was The Grassington Murderer?

THE GRASSINGTON MURDER:
THE STORY OF THE INFAMOUS TOM LEE

"How dreadful the fate of the wretches who fall,
A victim to laws they have broke!
Of vice, the beginning is frequently small,
But how fatal at length is the stroke!
The contents of these volumes will amply display,
The steps which offenders have trod:
Learn hence, then, each reader, the laws to obey
of your Country, your King and your God."

This rhyme was published in the Tyburn Chronicle in 1769 as a stark warning, lest any reader should be tempted to follow in the footsteps of Tom Lee, and contemplate any of the following crimes:

'Bigamy, Murders, Riots, Forgeries, Perjury, Sodomy, Piracy, Highway-Robberies, Starving, House-Breaking, Rapes, Treason, and other most enormous crimes of Villainy display'd in all its branches.'

The tale of Tom Lee is a something of a legend in the Upper Wharfedale district of Yorkshire. That it is true is indisputable. There is sound documentary evidence describing the events that took place. However, that the most well-known and most believed version of the story is entirely true is perhaps more doubtful. Later renderings of historical events tend by their own nature to evolve, become exaggerated, or are corrupted by the values and fashions of their time. Often, the actual chain of events becomes secondary to the desire to entertain the audience of the time. Coupled with the unavoidable effect of 'Chinese whispers' and the inevitable desire of the storyteller to deliver a rounded, entertaining, and complete tale to his or her audience, it is perhaps not surprising that the one version of the Tom Lee saga to achieve all those things has become the accepted standard – one on which all later retellings are based.

1766 was a volatile year. Just twenty-one years after the Jacobite rebellion in Scotland, the exiled Prince Charles Edward Stuart still yearned for the British throne, hoping to be crowned King Charles III. In the American colonies, British forces continued to quell 'Yankee' uprisings and discontent, while the slave trade saw ever more densely packed ships plying their grim trade across the busy sea lanes of the Atlantic.

Meanwhile, In Upper Wharfedale, life continued very much as it had for many years. Women busied themselves domestically, praying that their husbands would not squander their meagre income from the lead mine on drink or gambling. Life was undoubtedly healthier in the fresh air of the less populated Dales than in the claustrophobic and unsanitary atmosphere of the crowded cities but, for all that, life was none the safer.

Crime was rife in rural England. Even by 1766 the West Riding of Yorkshire was still eighty years away from a unified and recognisable police force. Each town or district employed a local constable, responsible for the collection of fines imposed by the local magistrates, or for undertaking such law enforcement tasks as deemed necessary by that magistrate, or in some instances, by an aggrieved landowner. The constable's salary was paid from a local levy, often in tied accommodation and food, rather than in shillings and pence. These officers received no formal training, had little in the way of protection or equipment – other than perhaps a handy stick or truncheon (known as a 'life preserver') – and often risked danger to life and limb far above and beyond that which would be acceptable today.

Highwaymen (such as the infamous Dick Turpin who had been executed in York just thirty years earlier) lurked in the shadows next to unseen stretches of the public roads, and vagabonds and travelling gypsies robbed unsuspecting travellers along the windy country lanes. Even in the busy market towns such as Grassington, pickpockets plied their trade among the unsuspecting crowds on market day and, as night fell, burglars jemmied open doors and even climbed down chimneys in pursuit of their ill-gotten gains. With none of our modern crime fighting techniques, forensic science, or even simple advantages like streetlighting, the odds in eighteenth-century England definitely favoured the criminal. In an attempt to counteract this imbalance, punishments were necessarily harsh. Gradually, by way of deterrent, the number of crimes for which a person could be executed increased dramatically. Known as 'The Bloody Code' the number of offences which carried with them the death penalty increased from fifty in 1688 to a mammoth 215 by 1815. These included crimes ranging from murder and arson, at one end of the scale, to wrecking a fishpond, destroying a turnpike road, or wearing a blackened face, at the other end.

Yet, these severe penalties did little to dissuade recidivists from continuing their criminal activities. The risk of being caught, weighed against the harshness of the sentences, seemed a gamble worth taking . . .

The Grassington Murder is available from bookshops, online, and via the authors website
www.markbridgemanauthor.co.uk

Companion books to *The Dark Side of the Dales*, also by Mark Bridgeman

The Grassington Murder
Fact or Fiction? The story of Tom Lee, the notorious
Grassington murderer and highwayman.
Available in paperback and ebook
£9.99

Blood Beneath Ben Nevis
True Stories of Murder, Myth and Mystery
from Lochaber.
£9.99

Erased
A collection of seven mysterious missing person
stories from around the world.
Available in paperback and ebook
£9.99

Perthshire's Pound of Flesh
More true Stories of Murder, Mystery and Deception
from Perth and Perthshire's Dark Past.
£9.99

Blood Across The Water
Blood, Brutality and Betrayal
True stories form the Highlands of Scotland.
£9.99

Mark's titles are available from all good bookshops,
online retailers, or via www.markbridgemanauthor.co.uk